JESUS:
the life changer

Simon Robinson

DayOne

© Day One Publications 2009.
Revised edition. First published in 2003.

Scripture quotations are from The New International Version unless otherwise stated.
© 1973, 1978, 1984, International Bible Society. Published by Hodder and Stoughton.

British Library Cataloguing in Publication Data available
ISBN 978-1-84625-123-8

Published by Day One Publications
Ryelands Road, Leominster, HR6 8NZ
TEL 01568 613 740   FAX 01568 611 473
email—sales@dayone.co.uk
web site—www.dayone.co.uk
North American e-mail—usasales@dayone.co.uk
North American web site—www.dayonebookstore.com

All rights reserved

No part of this publication may be reproduced, or stored in a retrieval system, or transmitted, in any form or by any means, mechanical, electronic, photocopying, recording or otherwise, without the prior permission of Day One Publications.

Cover design by Wayne McMaster and printed by Orchard Press Cheltenham Ltd.

Dedication
To my sons,
Andrew and Matthew

COMMENDATIONS

'Simon Robinson paints with words. In his book he uses telling brushstrokes to reveal a panoramic view of the life of Jesus, as seen through the eyes of some of the lesser-known characters in the Bible. Simon has an eye for words and a heart for truth. Reading his book was like wandering through an art gallery, savouring new and fresh perspectives on the great masterpieces of faith—redemption, hope, love, and ultimately Jesus himself. Stare into Simon's word-painting and you'll come away with a new picture of Jesus.'

Terry Esau, Surprise Me/Nudge The World, LLC

'This is Christian teaching at its most creative; I found myself inspired time and again by Simon Robinson's wonderfully fresh angle on the gospel stories.'

Rico Tice, Associate Minister, All Souls, Langham Place, London

'What would it be like to meet some of the people who met Jesus—those who saw him, spoke to him and had their lives changed by him? Simon Robinson's delightful, imaginative and faithful amplifications of biblical stories bring these characters from the past alive. And what would it be like to meet Jesus today—to have your life changed by him? Read this book and let Jesus come alive to you.'

Christopher Cocksworth, Bishop of Coventry

AUTHOR'S NOTE

This book creatively tells the stories of people who met Jesus as if in their own words. We know the names of some of these people because they are recorded for us in the Bible, but other names have been made up. Names that are made up are marked by an asterisk. Each encounter is followed by the Bible passage on which it is based and some study questions to help you explore the biblical account. If you are not a Christian, you might find it helpful to go through these questions with a Christian friend.

CONTENTS

1	THE RETURN OF THE NATIVE	8
2	A SIGN IN THE SKY	14
3	THE FINAL WORD	20
4	THE WEDDING GUEST	26
5	AN OFFER TO AN OUTCAST	32
6	DESPERATE MEASURES	38
7	LOST AND FOUND	44
8	A SHEPHERD IN THE WILDERNESS	50
9	A TRAVELLER'S TALE	56
10	THE KING BREAKS IN	62
11	A CONFLICT IN THE CRYPT	68
12	A VIEW FROM THE SHADOWS	74
13	A DIARY OF MY DISAPPOINTMENT	80
14	AN INNOCENT MAN	86
15	DRAMA ON DEATH ROW	92
16	THE CASE OF THE TORN CURTAIN	98
17	FROM DESPERATION TO CELEBRATION	104
18	A CHANGE OF TONE	114
19	A LOOK BACK IN WONDER	120
	ENDNOTES	126

1 The return of the native

By **Jonas Bartholomew***

Green in winter, gold in summer: to me, those hills always seemed like sentries guarding our town. At last, I was strong enough to get to the top. Each footstep was purposefully planted, and any trace of fatigue was washed away by anticipation at what lay at the top. The climb got steeper, but then began to level off. I ran the rest of the way, longing to see what was beyond it. A huge lake lay in the distance, other villages were scattered across the landscape, sheep were grazing on the hillside, and farmers were working in their fields. There was a world out there, and one day I was going to explore it for myself! I wasn't going to stay in this little town all my life. Now that I had defeated those hills, I was going to escape and live my life to the full.

Twenty years later, my childhood dream lies in tatters. I have a small business that gets me a reasonable living but it gives me no excitement. I have climbed that hill many times since I first conquered it in my childhood, but now I do so with a sense of disappointment. Life seems to be mapped out for me—I'll work to keep my business going, get married, raise some children and die.

> **Most of the people I grew up with have settled in our small town, but one man seems to have broken free.**

Most of the people I grew up with have settled in our small town, but one man seems to have broken free. We grew up together and were trained in our fathers' trade, which was carpentry. I had always assumed that our lives would run a parallel course. But then he left town and, a little later, there were reports that he had been travelling around the villages, attracting huge crowds, enthralling them with his stories and performing miracles. It seemed hard to believe that we had spent our childhood together; what was so different about him?

Saturday finally came round. It was a welcome relief from the sweat and toil of my workshop, a chance to relax, take stock of life and feel human again. This particular Saturday began as any other. I woke up an hour later than usual, took longer over breakfast and went to the place of worship. After closing the door of my house, I joined a group of friends who were heading in the same direction. We exchanged news, shared opinions and swapped gossip. As we walked into the building, a familiar silence descended upon us. Smiles turned to serious expressions, and laughs to nervous coughs; this wasn't a time for levity, it was a time to be serious. The man at the front welcomed us, picked up several scrolls and handed them out to be read aloud. The first went back to the early days of our people, telling us about the experience of our ancestors who lived in the desert. The second contained some words from our law. A visitor read the third, and when I realized who he was, a surge of excitement swept through me. He was the man who had left town and had been attracting huge crowds. Every eye was riveted on him as he stood up to speak. The reading could hardly have been any more relevant. It was all about God's servant, who had come to tell prisoners they would be free, give sight to the blind, release the oppressed and declare that it was a time of God's favour.[1]

As he spoke, images of our childhood days were flashing through my mind, all sorts of questions about him were wriggling around my head, and while all this was going on, I tried my hardest to concentrate on the words he was reading. He read in a way I had never heard before; his voice carried authority, conviction and urgency. When he had finished, he rolled up the scroll, handed it to the attendant, looked straight at us and said, 'This has been fulfilled today while you have been listening.'

He read in a way I had never heard before; his voice carried authority, conviction and urgency.

When the service had finished, there was not the usual hum of conversation: the atmosphere was subdued and the discussion serious. It was confined to one subject—the man who had just read to us. Everyone seemed to be impressed by him and many people commented on the authority with which he spoke. However, because he had grown up in our town, they wanted to see him perform a miracle before they'd give any more thought to what he had been saying.

It was as though he knew what was going on in their minds.

It was as though he knew what was going on in their minds. 'I expect you'll quote that proverb to me—the one that says "physician, heal yourself". What you're really saying is, "Why don't you do the same kinds of miracles you performed in those other towns?" But the fact is that no prophet is accepted in his home town.' He went on to recall two occasions in our history when God had used a prophet to show his favour to outsiders instead of to our own people. This infuriated them: 'How dare he say that others are more favoured than we are!' They said to one another, 'After all, we are the people of God—others will never know him as we do.' They were seething with rage and they pressed in around him, forcing him to walk up to the top of the hill. When they had got him to the peak, they had every intention of pushing him off, but he walked right through the crowd and left.

Who was this man? His name is Jesus—a person you cannot be neutral about. Some people say that he has turned their lives upside down, others bay for his blood, but everyone has an opinion about him. In the chapters that follow, we're going to get the inside story from people who have met with him and have been changed by him.

JESUS returned to Galilee in the power of the Spirit, and news about him spread through the whole countryside. He taught in their synagogues, and everyone praised him.

He went to Nazareth, where he had been brought up, and on the Sabbath day he went into the synagogue, as was his custom. And he stood up to read. The scroll of the prophet Isaiah was handed to him. Unrolling it, he found the place where it is written: 'The Spirit of the Lord is on me, because he has anointed me to preach good news to the poor. He has sent me to proclaim freedom for the prisoners and recovery of sight for the blind, to release the oppressed, to proclaim the year of the Lord's favour.'

Then he rolled up the scroll, gave it back to the attendant and sat down. The eyes of everyone in the synagogue were fastened on him, and he began by saying to them, 'Today this scripture is fulfilled in your hearing.'

All spoke well of him and were amazed at the gracious words that came from his lips. 'Isn't this Joseph's son?' they asked.

Jesus said to them, 'Surely you will quote this proverb to me: "Physician, heal yourself! Do here in your home town what we have heard that you did in Capernaum."'

'I tell you the truth,' he continued, 'no prophet is accepted in his home town. I assure you that there were many widows in Israel in Elijah's time, when the sky was shut for three and a half years and there was a severe famine throughout the land. Yet Elijah was not sent to any of them, but to a widow in Zarephath in the region of Sidon. And there were many in Israel with leprosy in the time of Elisha the prophet, yet not one of them was cleansed—only Naaman the Syrian.'

All the people in the synagogue were furious when they heard this. They got up, drove him out of the town, and took him to the brow of the hill on which the town was built, in order to throw him down the cliff. But he walked right through the crowd and went on his way. (Luke 4:14–30)

Think it through!

- Why didn't these people accept Jesus?
- Why did they get angry with Him?
- Do you think He would get the same response today?

MORE STUDY QUESTIONS ➤

- Luke said that, after Jesus had rolled up the scroll and handed it back to the attendant, He said, 'This Scripture is fulfilled in your hearing.' What was the passage He read from about?
- How did Jesus fulfil it?
- What does this tell us about Jesus' approach to the Old Testament?
- Can we know about Jesus without the Bible?
- Jesus has been described as 'a person you cannot be neutral about'. Honestly assess your own reaction to Him.

2 A sign in the sky

By **Akbar al-Kadar***

Daylight has never held much appeal for me; I love the night. As a small child, I used to look away from the closeness of my mother's face to the distance of the small bright lights in the sky. As I grew up, I shunned the energetic games my friends would play and hid myself in my room studying charts of the stars. At night, I would spend many hours lying on my back looking at the sky. The stars have been my passion for as long as I can remember. They take my mind out of the confined spaces of this world into the great expanse of the unknown and onto the great force behind them. They make me realize how little I know, how great this universe is, and how much more of it there is to discover. During the day, the sky is predictable—if it is clear, the sun shines; if it is covered with thick cloud, we expect rain. But when darkness spreads its cloak, the unexpected happens. A familiar light evaporates, a new cluster of stars and constellations takes its place, and sometimes a long bright light may paint a streak through the dense blackness.

The stars have been my life's work, from the simple charts I consulted as a boy to the complex analyses I was taught at the seminary. They have occupied my waking hours and even broken into my dreams. The world around me has changed rapidly, rulers have risen and fallen, empires have come and gone, people have lived and died. But if I could understand what is going on in the sky, I might be able to comprehend the mind of the one who puts the stars in their places and ignites the massive spheres of fire that I have seen hurtling through the atmosphere.

A while ago, speculation about a great King emerging from Judea began to spread through the region. At first, I took little notice—until I heard people talk about the stars. For centuries, the Jews, who have suffered defeat, invasion and captivity, have cherished something in their sacred writings. They told them that a star would come and herald the arrival of a great King. The whispers became more audible, and the number of people talking about this increased. It could be a chance for me to gain some insight into the mind of the one who rules the sky.

If I could understand what is going on in the sky, I might be able to comprehend the mind of the one who puts the stars in their places.

Recently, I was scanning the night sky when I saw a star that shone more intensely and moved across the atmosphere more elegantly than any I had ever seen. I was certain that it was the one spoken about in the Jews' sacred writings. I quickly gathered my colleagues and showed them the constellation, urging them to come and search for the King whose arrival it announced. They shared my excitement and enthused about joining me, but they all asked what we should be doing next. There was silence; I stroked my chin as I thought about it. 'Let's use logic,' I said. 'Surely if he is to be the King of the Jews, we should travel to Jerusalem.' Everyone agreed, and we began to make preparations for the long journey.

After many scorching days and freezing nights travelling across the inhospitable desert terrain, we arrived in Jerusalem and began to ask people if they knew anything about the new King. Their reaction was surprising; they seemed to be suspicious of us and fearful of Herod (the man the Romans had put in place to rule over them). We had almost given up hope of getting any further when an envoy crept into our lodgings with a message from Herod himself saying that he wanted to speak to us privately.

We were not to see him until night fell, but as soon as it did, the envoy led us a different way into the city and took us to Herod's palace. I have never met a king before, but just on first impression I could tell that this man had the authority and ruthlessness necessary to rule people. He greeted us warmly: 'Welcome, travellers,' he said in a booming voice, 'you have come many miles to be here. You must know a lot about this King you speak of. Tell me how you first heard about him and what you know of him.' He seemed so amiable towards us and interested in what we had to say that we held nothing back and told him everything we knew. This delighted him. 'Good, good,' he said, placing his hand on my shoulder, 'then you must go and search for him and return to tell me more. My envoy will lead you back to your lodgings and you should start your journey as soon as you can.'

We planned to leave the next morning,

Jesus: the life changer

but just as we were about to enter our lodgings I saw that same extraordinary light in the sky that began this chain of events. I called out to the others, 'It's the star again, the one their sacred writings speak about; it must be leading us to the King. Let's follow it!'

We travelled north until we arrived at a town called Bethlehem, where the star stopped above a house.

It wasn't the kind of place I would have associated with a King.

It wasn't the kind of place I would have associated with a King: just an ordinary home that had been illuminated by an extraordinary light in the sky. I knocked on the door and was greeted by someone who appeared to be a Jewish craftsman. He didn't seem the slightest bit surprised that a group of foreign visitors were standing at his door. 'Sir,' I said, pointing to the sky, 'we have followed this star to find a King promised in your sacred writings and it has led us to your home.' He smiled in a way that told me he knew exactly what I was talking about and led us into the house. He pointed to a young child and said, 'Here is the one you are looking for.'

To take my mind away from the hardship of the journey, I had tried to picture what the King would look like. I had imagined him to be well dressed and stately-looking, surrounded by servants who were ready to act on his every whim. But he was an ordinary boy living in a simple home with disadvantaged parents. Yet something indescribable seemed to radiate through the ordinary bundle of young humanity standing in front of me; in fact, it was something that made me think about the one who made the stars. We all stood in silence, offered him our gifts and, without any prompting, bowed down in worship. We were not Jews, but we all realized that he was our King, too.

I slept fitfully that night, restless from the excitement of our discovery, wondering what this boy would grow up to do and what kind of an impact it would have on the world. When I managed to get to sleep, I had a dream in which the one who made the stars spoke to me, warning me that, out of jealousy and fear, Herod wanted to kill the boy, and that I should travel home another way.

I still scrutinize the night sky and study the stars, and I have never seen anything like the one that led me to Bethlehem. But I am sure that he who made the stars will use this King in a way that eclipses the wonder of that dazzling light in the sky that had led me to such an extraordinary discovery.

NOW after Jesus was born in Bethlehem of Judea in the days of Herod the king, behold, wise men from the East came to Jerusalem, saying, 'Where is He who has been born King of the Jews? For we have seen His star in the East and have come to worship Him.' When Herod the king heard this, he was troubled, and all Jerusalem with him. And when he had gathered all the chief priests and scribes of the people together, he inquired of them where the Christ was to be born. So they said to him, 'In Bethlehem of Judea, for thus it is written by the prophet: "But you, Bethlehem, in the land of Judah, Are not the least among the rulers of Judah; For out of you shall come a Ruler Who will shepherd My people Israel."' Then Herod, when he had secretly called the wise men, determined from them what time the star appeared. And he sent them to Bethlehem and said, 'Go and search carefully for the young Child, and when you have found Him, bring back word to me, that I may come and worship Him also.' When they heard the king, they departed; and behold, the star which they had seen in the East went before them, till it came and stood over where the young Child was. When they saw the star, they rejoiced with exceedingly great joy. And when they had come into the house, they saw the young Child with Mary His mother, and fell down and worshipped Him. And when they had opened their treasures, they presented gifts to Him: gold, frankincense, and myrrh. Then, being divinely warned in a dream that they should not return to Herod, they departed for their own country another way. (Matthew 2:1–12, New King James Version)

Think it through!

- Which two sources of information did the wise men have about the King they searched for?

- What is surprising about these men looking for the 'King of the Jews'?

MORE STUDY QUESTIONS ▶

Jesus: the life changer

➢ What does this tell us about the scope of Jesus' rule?

➢ Why was Herod so disturbed at the wise men's quest to find 'the King of the Jews'?

➢ Where was Jesus when they finally found Him? How does this differ from the scenes in Christmas cards and nativity plays?

➢ What is the importance of these 'wise men from the East' searching for 'the King of the Jews'?

3 The final word

By **John the Baptist**

I have always felt different from the people around me. I first became aware of this when I was a child; everyone else's parents were young and active, while mine were old and frail. My friends spent time in their fathers' workshops learning a trade, while my father spent time teaching me in the Temple. Their parents used to go to a place of worship, while my father led them in worship. But there was more to it than that: since I had the ability to form thoughts and ideas in my mind, I have been aware of a sense of destiny. When I asked my father why he was so much older than my friends' parents, he'd smile wistfully and tell me that I was a wonderful gift from God, describing my mother's heartache at not having any children. 'Your poor mother used to cry herself to sleep because she had no child to care for, and the good Lord heard her cry.' As I grew older, he told me more.

'I had waited years and years to serve in the Most Holy part of the Temple. At last I was chosen, and I can't tell you how privileged I felt. I began to burn the incense, and while the crowd stayed outside, I was praying and thanking God for the privilege he had given me. Suddenly, I became aware that someone else was standing near me. As I turned around, I could feel the hairs on the back of my neck stand on end—it was an angel!'

He described the scene so vividly that I felt as if I was in the Temple when the visitor had come. 'What did the angel say to you, father?' I asked.

A serious expression suddenly came across his face. 'Son,' he said, as he laid his hand on my shoulder, 'you must listen to me very carefully, because I am only going to tell this to you once.' My eyes widened as I strained to hear every last syllable of what he was about to say. 'The angel told me that you were going to be born. He said that many people would rejoice at your birth, that you would be great in God's eyes, and that you would be like the Prophet Elijah—a man who had God's Spirit upon him.'

> **'He said that many people would rejoice at your birth, that you would be great in God's eyes, and that you would be like the Prophet Elijah.'**

I knew I was different, but I could hardly take this in. 'Me, father, but why?' I asked. He looked a little annoyed that I had stopped him, and breathed deeply, his frame rising and falling with his breath. 'You have a mission from God,' he said, punctuating his words by nodding his head. 'You will persuade many people to turn to the Lord, and you will prepare them for the arrival of the new King spoken of by the Prophets.' I found this news exhilarating, but my excitement was soon punctured by a very sober tone in my father's voice. 'The angel also told me that you must never touch wine or strong drink because even before your birth you would be filled with the Holy Spirit.'

Then he cut off eye contact with me, looked to the floor and said, 'I am ashamed to say that I didn't believe him. I told him that I thought your mother and I were too old to have a child, and expressed doubt about the whole thing, and the next thing I knew was that I was struck dumb. "I am Gabriel!" the angel said. "I stand in the very presence of God. It was he who sent me to bring you this good news! And now, since you didn't believe what I said, you won't be able to speak until the child is born. For my words will certainly come true at the proper time."[2] When your mother found she was expecting a child, she was ecstatic, but I was not able to say anything to echo her joy until you were eight days old, when it was time to name you. Our friends and relatives encouraged your mother to name you after me, but I waved my hands in protest and wrote down the name the angel told me to give you, and at that moment my speech returned. News of this spread around the district like wildfire, and people asked one another what kind of a man you would grow up to be.'

It has been many years since my father and I had that conversation. I have never lost the sense of destiny but God has led me in a way I didn't expect. I spend most of my time in the heat and haze of the desert where I have been preaching to people—calling them to turn away from their sins to God, who will forgive them. I have been immersing them in the river as a sign that they have responded

Jesus: the life changer

to the message and have been cleansed from their sins. I dress in simple clothes suitable for the desert and I eat the only food this inhospitable region yields: wild honey and locusts. You may wonder how this fits in with the great things my father told me about, but you have to be here to understand the amazing things that are happening. Thousands of people have been leaving the shade and security of the towns and have taken to the desert road to hear and respond to the message God has given me. Just the other day, I even had a delegation of religious leaders from Jerusalem visit me. They asked me if I was Elijah or a Prophet, and I told them that I was neither. 'Tell us who you are, and then we'll be able to give an answer to the people who sent us.' 'All right,' I replied, 'I'll answer you from the Scriptures: I am "a voice shouting in the wilderness, 'Prepare a pathway for the Lord's coming.'"'[3]

It was not enough for them. 'If you are not the King which the Prophets spoke of, or Elijah, or the Prophet, then what right do you have to immerse these people in water and declare that God has forgiven their sins?' At this point, the training my father had given me was very useful. I quickly reviewed my options. Should I talk about the promises God had given to us in the Prophets' writings? Should I explain why it is so important that we prepare for the King's arrival by turning to God and asking him to forgive our sins? Should I confront them, as I had done with others, and call them 'a brood of vipers'?[4] I paused, prayed, and thought very carefully, then I gave them an answer that I am certain God put in my mind. 'There is someone else about to come on the scene—someone so great that I would not be worthy to perform the most menial task for him. And while I can only immerse you in water, he will immerse you with the Holy Spirit, and my work anticipates this.'

Day after day, as the crowds flocked to the desert, I scanned the horizon to see if I could catch a sight of the one I spoke about. What would he look like? How would I recognize him? What should I say to him? At last, a figure appeared on the horizon who filled me with a sense of expectancy—he wore no crown, and he had no army marching behind him, but he was a man, and he was none other than my cousin Jesus. 'Look!' I bellowed out to everyone around. 'This man is like the lamb we offer to God in order that we may be forgiven for our sins. He is *the* Lamb of God and he will take away the sins of the world. He is the one I have been telling you about.'

My destiny was fulfilled, my work was finished and I was ready to hand everything over to him when he made a request which took me completely by surprise. 'I want you to immerse me in the water, John,' he said. I didn't know quite what to say. 'Surely this cannot be right,' I protested, 'you should be immersing me!' But he was adamant: 'This is the way it has to be done, because we must do everything that is right.'

> **I was ready to hand everything over to him when he made a request which took me completely by surprise.**

I abandoned my protest, dropped my head and nodded. Putting my hand on his shoulder, I led Jesus into the river and then lowered him beneath the water. As he came up, it was as if a window in heaven had been opened to shed light on him. Suddenly, a dove appeared and rested on Jesus.[5] My mind went back to something my father had read to me from the Scriptures about the time when God had flooded the world. At the end of the ordeal, the people God had kept safe—Noah and his family—sent out a dove to check that the flood had finally receded. It marked a new beginning for the world—just like the arrival of Jesus, here in the desert. God had kept his promise and sent us a King; a new day had dawned.

Then I heard a voice unlike any I have heard before: it was awesome, yet comforting; foreboding, yet encouraging; from time, yet from eternity. It was God's voice. 'This is my beloved son,' he said, 'and I am fully pleased with him.'[6] The man who stood before me, dripping with water, was God's final word to us.

Jesus: the life changer

IN those days John the Baptist came, preaching in the Desert of Judea and saying, 'Repent, for the kingdom of heaven is near.' This is he who was spoken of through the prophet Isaiah: 'A voice of one calling in the desert, "Prepare the way for the Lord, make straight paths for him."'

John's clothes were made of camel's hair, and he had a leather belt round his waist. His food was locusts and wild honey. People went out to him from Jerusalem and all Judea and the whole region of the Jordan. Confessing their sins, they were baptised by him in the Jordan River.

But when he saw many of the Pharisees and Sadducees coming to where he was baptising, he said to them: 'You brood of vipers! Who warned you to flee from the coming wrath? Produce fruit in keeping with repentance. And do not think you can say to yourselves, "We have Abraham as our father." I tell you that out of these stones God can raise up children for Abraham. The axe is already at the root of the trees, and every tree that does not produce good fruit will be cut down and thrown into the fire.

'I baptise you with water for repentance. But after me will come one who is more powerful than I, whose sandals I am not fit to carry. He will baptise you with the Holy Spirit and with fire. His winnowing fork is in his hand, and he will clear his threshing-floor, gathering his wheat into the barn and burning up the chaff with unquenchable fire.'

Then Jesus came from Galilee to the Jordan to be baptised by John. But John tried to deter him, saying, 'I need to be baptised by you, and do you come to me?'

Jesus replied, 'Let it be so now; it is proper for us to do this to fulfil all righteousness.' Then John consented.

As soon as Jesus was baptised, he went up out of the water. At that moment heaven was opened, and he saw the Spirit of God descending like a dove and lighting on him. And a voice from heaven said, 'This is my Son, whom I love; with him I am well pleased.' (Matthew 3:1–17)

Think it through!

- What was John the Baptist's role?
- What did people do before they were baptised?

Jesus: the life changer

- Why does John tell the religious leaders (Pharisees and Sadducees) to 'produce fruit in keeping with repentance'? What did he mean?
- Who was the one to come after John?
- What did John mean when he said, 'I baptise you with water for repentance. But … he will baptise you with the Holy Spirit and with fire'?
- What were the warnings he gave about Jesus?
- Why did Jesus want to be baptised by John?
- Think about the significance of the Holy Spirit descending upon Jesus and the words spoken by His Father as He came up out of the water.

Jesus: the life changer

4 The wedding guest

By **Shaul Bacharias***

Some people thrive on organization. They are able to turn chaos into order, uncertainty into expectation, and unease into confidence. And at a time like this, I wish I were such a person! It is the night before my wedding, and there are so many things needing to be done that I don't know whether I am coming or going.

In our culture, the bridegroom is responsible for arranging his wedding. It is looked on as the first test of his ability to care for his wife and manage his home. If everything goes smoothly, friends and family will heap praises on him, but if something goes wrong, he suffers a sense of deep shame, and will be told that he has let everyone down. Most of my friends are already married; their weddings were faultless, and they assure me it is easy. But as I wipe my brow and try to make something of the chaos around me, I have a sinking feeling that I am going to have a very different experience. I have gone through what needs to be done in my mind and everything seems to be covered. I have arranged the service, booked the hall for the reception, hired caterers, and paid for a Steward, who will make all the announcements and supervise the reception. Plenty of food and drink has been ordered, transport has been laid on and guests have been invited. It looks as if I have done all I need to do, but I still feel nervous.

> **It looks as if I have done all I need to do, but I still feel nervous.**

One of the things nagging away at me is the uncertainty about how long the celebrations will last. I have been to weddings that have gone on for anything from a day to a week; what if my guests enjoy themselves so much they stay for days on end and we run out of food or drink?

Now five days have passed, and there is so much to write about! I have taken my new wife back to my home, and I am basking in a sense of relief that the wedding was successful, and joy that I am finally married. It was not without its difficulties, though. Let me tell you what happened.

I woke up early, my stomach knotted up and my head spinning. I sat up in bed and breathed deeply a few times, trying to remind myself that the most important thing about today was not the practical arrangements but the commitment I was making to the girl who was to be my wife. I began to review the things that should have been done but decided that there was no point; if I had forgotten something, it was too late to do anything about it. Hopefully, everything was organized.

Too nervous to be hungry, I picked at my breakfast, and pushed away my plate with most of the food left uneaten. I was too immersed in my thoughts to hear my friend's footsteps as he approached the house, so he took me by surprise when he let himself in. 'Good morning, Bridegroom! I hope you have everything ready—we'll need to leave shortly.' I frowned and said, 'I just hope I haven't left anything out—you know that organization is not my strongest point.' My friend was one of those people who know exactly what to say to reassure me. 'Don't worry,' he said, putting his hand on my shoulder, 'you have checked everything; what could possibly go wrong?' I muttered a few incoherent words and went to change into my wedding clothes.

I wanted everything to be just right, so it took me longer than usual to change, and I could hear people gathering outside my house. They had come to join our procession to the bride's home. 'Hurry up,' shouted my friend, 'it's almost time to leave.' A few minutes later, I stepped out, smart, confident and happy. This was going to be a very special day for me and I was determined not to let anything spoil it, so I was going to put my worries out of my mind. I led the procession, winding through the narrow streets, waving to well-wishers and enjoying the attention we were attracting. Once we stepped onto the road where my bride and her parents lived, we slowed down, until we stopped outside their house. It was my friend's duty to make a formal announcement. He knocked on the door, calling out the name of my future father-in-law. 'I have the bridegroom with me, and he asks for his bride.' The door creaked open and the bride's father appeared, his daughter on his arm dressed in a sumptuous wedding gown and covered in jewels that dazzled in the morning sun. She stood by my side, her attendants came behind us and, to the sound of singing, we made our way to the place where we were to be married.

After the wedding, the guests followed us to the place where we were to have our celebration. My heart swelled with satisfaction when I saw the lavish meal that had been set out. The Steward looked in my direction, waiting for me to give the word for the feast to begin. I nodded, and he called out for silence. The excited hum of the crowd subsided. 'Friends, eat and drink, for this is a time to be happy!' he shouted. The rest of the day seems a blur; my bride was beautiful, my guests were satisfied, and my worries seemed to be groundless. Between our frequent bouts of eating and drinking, people sang, read out love poems and told stories. Everyone who spoke to me congratulated me for organizing such a great wedding.

The celebration lasted several days. Some people stayed with us the whole time, but others went out to work and came back in the evening. At the end of the second day, my worries had evaporated; things could not be going better. The drawback was that the guests were enjoying themselves so much that they were in no hurry to leave, and by the third day the wine had run out. The room was no longer vibrant with songs and laughter: it rumbled with the unhappy noise of complaint, and I felt overwhelmed with a sense of shame. I had let down my new wife and my guests.

I felt overwhelmed with a sense of shame. I had let down my new wife and my guests.

A woman and her son were locked in deep conversation. I had noticed them earlier; her son seemed to stand out from the other guests. 'Can't you do anything for that man?' she said. I wondered what it was he could do; perhaps he was a wine trader and was able to get hold of some fresh supplies quickly. But he did not give his mother a positive answer. 'My time has not come yet,' he said. The woman did not take this as a 'no' and, without saying any more to her son, she turned to the caterers, telling them to do whatever her son told them. At the back of the hall were six big containers; the son pointed to them and told the caterers to fill them with water. What good did he think that would do? I could not see the guests drinking water after they had been enjoying good wine for the last three days. When the last container was full, he told one of them to fill a cup from it and take it to the Steward. I am not sure whether I was bemused or horrified by this; what was he trying to do—add to my embarrassment? With an air of resignation, I watched the caterer walk to the other side of the room. The Steward took the cup of water, smelt it (as if it were wine), sampled it and, to my astonishment, nodded with approval. Then he looked over to me, lifting the cup in the air. 'This wine is excellent!' he shouted. 'Most people would use it up at the beginning of the celebration, but you've saved the best until now!' The mood changed, the guests cheered, and my shame had gone.

Until recently, this woman's son had been a local carpenter, and since my wedding, everyone seems to be talking about him. He travels around doing miracles and speaking about a Kingdom that God is going to establish; some people say that he is the King promised by God. Now my wedding is over, I have given these events a lot of thought.

His words remind me of some promises God gave the Prophets centuries ago.

The Steward congratulated me for saving the best wine until last and, as far as he was concerned, he was passing comment on my taste in wine. But his words remind me of some promises God gave the Prophets centuries ago; promises that 'the vats will overflow with new wine and oil',[7] and that 'new wine will drip from the mountains'.[8] This man turned water into wine! Surely he has brought these promises into reality! But why did he tell his mother that his hour had not yet come? The look in his eyes and the tone of his voice showed a sense of destiny. He knows that something very important lies in the distance. What can it be? From now on, I will follow his movements with great interest.

Jesus: the life changer **29**

ON the third day a wedding took place at Cana in Galilee. Jesus' mother was there, and Jesus and his disciples had also been invited to the wedding. When the wine was gone, Jesus' mother said to him, 'They have no more wine.'

'Dear woman, why do you involve me?' Jesus replied. 'My time has not yet come.'

His mother said to the servants, 'Do whatever he tells you.'

Nearby stood six stone water jars, the kind used by the Jews for ceremonial washing, each holding from twenty to thirty gallons.

Jesus said to the servants, 'Fill the jars with water'; so they filled them to the brim.

Then he told them, 'Now draw some out and take it to the master of the banquet.'

They did so, and the master of the banquet tasted the water that had been turned into wine. He did not realise where it had come from, though the servants who had drawn the water knew. Then he called the bridegroom aside and said, 'Everyone brings out the choice wine first and then the cheaper wine after the guests have had too much to drink; but you have saved the best till now.'

This, the first of his miraculous signs, Jesus performed in Cana of Galilee. He thus revealed his glory, and his disciples put their faith in him. (John 2:1–11)

Think it through!

➢ What does this event tell us about Jesus' sense of purpose?

➢ To whom did He see Himself accountable?

- What is the irony of the master of the banquet saying, 'Everyone brings out the choice wine first and then the cheaper wine after the guests have had too much to drink; but you have saved the best till now'?

- Read the following verses. How does this miracle fulfil promises made in them?

  > 'The days are coming,' declares the Lord, 'when the reaper will be overtaken by the ploughman and the planter by the one treading grapes. New wine will drip from the mountains and flow from all the hills.' (Amos 9:13)

  > 'Be glad, O people of Zion, rejoice in the Lord your God, for he has given you the autumn rains in righteousness. He sends you abundant showers, both autumn and spring rains, as before. The threshing floors will be filled with grain; the vats will overflow with new wine and oil.' (Joel 2:23–24)

5 An offer to an outcast

By **Leah of Samaria***

I was walking with my mother, excited about my first visit to the market, my sense of smell bombarded with the mingle of aromas and my mind busy taking in the new sights, when I saw a sad old man. The world around me seemed to come to a standstill. He was sitting by the roadside, his body disfigured by disease and his face wizened from life on the streets. It was his eyes that moved me the most. They were so sad and distant, reflecting year upon year of pain.

Who was he, and why was no one taking care of him? Surely mother would do something to help. But she acted as if he didn't exist. I tugged at her hand until she came to a halt. 'Mother, didn't you see that poor man? He looked so sad. Can't we do something to make him happy?' She looked round and gave the man a quick glance. 'Listen,' she said, with a harshness I hadn't heard before, 'if you ever see someone like that again, you mustn't even look at him; just walk on!'

That man must have long since died, but his eyes seem to have burned deep into my soul. And now that I have grown up, I can understand his pain, for I am an outcast too. I have been married five times, and I am living with a man who isn't my husband. When people see me in the street, they behave in the same way in which my mother acted towards the man I met all those years ago. They cross the street, look the other way, and get as far away from me as they can. Eventually, I decided to save myself any more pain. Each day, I would sneak into the market with my face covered so that no one would recognize me. That was the easy part—you can lose yourself in the crowd on market day—but the daily visit to collect my water supply was another matter. Clusters of people gathered around the cistern in the coolest part of the day, and they'd stop talking as soon as I arrived. I decided to collect my water in the blistering midday sun, when everyone else was taking shelter from it. I'd rather endure the scorching sun than the scorn of people!

It was a day like any other. I waited until noon, picked up my water carrier and ventured out into the shimmering heat. As I got closer, my heart sank; I could see a person sitting by the well. He was a man in his thirties. He looked tired, hot and thirsty, but he didn't have anything to draw water with. He was a stranger; in fact, he looked as if he came from across the border. I assumed that he must have lost his way because he came from a race who wouldn't go anywhere near mine. I tried not to look at him and got on with my task, but he seemed to have a presence about him. Who was he, and what was he doing sitting by a well in the hottest part of the day? Didn't he realize he was in territory which was inhabited by people who had been at loggerheads with his race for centuries?

> **I tried not to look at him and got on with my task, but he seemed to have a presence about him.**

I was too deep in thought to notice that the stranger had turned around to speak to me, so the sound of his voice made me jump. 'Would you give me a drink, please?' he asked. Being an outcast, I hadn't had much opportunity to develop the art of conversation, and I was so surprised to hear him speak that any social graces I might have possessed completely evaded me. I blurted out the first thing that came into my mind. 'You're from across the border! Why are you stooping to ask someone like me for a drink?' I thought this might bring the conversation to a swift conclusion, but the stranger wasn't deterred in the slightest. He took charge of the conversation and guided it in an unexpected direction. He spoke about a 'gift of God', and he told me that if I knew about this 'gift' and realized who I was speaking to, I could have asked him for 'living water'. The idea of water that had been freshly taken from a stream sounded like a dream in our arid climate. 'Listen,' I snapped, 'I'm the one with the jar, while you're sitting there, hot and thirsty! What makes you think you have something you can offer me?' But he wouldn't be put off. 'When people drink from this well, they'll get thirsty again. I'm going to give people a very different kind of water; it's going to put an end to thirst altogether. In fact, once people drink it, they will have their own spring inside them, which will give them eternal life.' I couldn't completely understand what he meant, but whatever this water was, I realized

Jesus: the life changer **33**

that it was something I needed. 'Please give me some,' I said rapidly, 'then I'll never get thirsty again.'

I was so engrossed in our discussion that I had lost all awareness of the oppressive noonday heat, but it came back when the stranger took the conversation in an unwelcome direction. 'Go and get your husband,' he said. He had touched a nerve and I wanted to get away from this subject as quickly as possible. 'I don't have one,' I replied. He looked me straight in the eye and said, 'I know that, but you've had husbands, haven't you? Five, to be precise. And you're not even married to the man you're living with now.'

> **The stranger knew everything about me. It made me feel very uncomfortable.**

I couldn't quite believe what I was hearing: the stranger knew everything about me. It made me feel very uncomfortable, so I tried to change the subject. 'Sir,' I said, with a new note of respect, 'I can see that you are some kind of a Prophet. Can you answer a question that has been bothering me for years? My people worship God at one place and your people at another; which of us is right?' But the stranger dismissed hundreds of years of debate by talking about something God was going to do in the future. 'Soon it won't matter where you go, because true children of God will worship their Father in spirit and in truth.' This reminded me of the promises God had given us through his Prophet. 'I know about the King that God has promised to send to us,' I said. 'He'll make it all clear when he comes!' Then came the most inspiring, invigorating words I had ever heard: 'I am the one you speak about,' he said. I ran into the village, forgetting my fear of meeting people in my eagerness to tell everyone about him. 'You must meet this man,' I shouted. 'He told me everything I ever did! Could he be the King promised by God?'

THE Pharisees heard that Jesus was gaining and baptising more disciples than John, although in fact it was not Jesus who baptised, but his disciples. When the Lord learned of this, he left Judea and went back once more to Galilee.

Now he had to go through Samaria. So he came to a town in Samaria called Sychar, near the plot of ground Jacob had given to his son Joseph. Jacob's well was there, and Jesus, tired as he was from the journey, sat down by the well. It was about the sixth hour.

When a Samaritan woman came to draw water, Jesus said to her, 'Will you give me a drink?' (His disciples had gone into the town to buy food.)

The Samaritan woman said to him, 'You are a Jew and I am a Samaritan woman. How can you ask me for a drink?' (For Jews do not associate with Samaritans.)

Jesus answered her, 'If you knew the gift of God and who it is that asks you for a drink, you would have asked him and he would have given you living water.'

'Sir,' the woman said, 'you have nothing to draw with and the well is deep. Where can you get this living water? Are you greater than our father Jacob, who gave us the well and drank from it himself, as did also his sons and his flocks and herds?'

Jesus answered, 'Everyone who drinks this water will be thirsty again, but whoever drinks the water I give him will never thirst. Indeed, the water I give him will become in him a spring of water welling up to eternal life.'

The woman said to him, 'Sir, give me this water so that I won't get thirsty and have to keep coming here to draw water.'

He told her, 'Go, call your husband and come back.'

'I have no husband,' she replied.

Jesus said to her, 'You are right when you say you have no husband. The fact is, you have had five husbands, and the man you now have is not your husband. What you have just said is quite true.'

'Sir,' the woman said, 'I can see that you are a prophet. Our fathers worshipped on this mountain, but you Jews claim that the place where we must worship is in Jerusalem.'

Jesus declared, 'Believe me, woman, a time is coming when you will worship the Father neither on this mountain nor in Jerusalem. You Samaritans worship what you do not know; we worship what we do know, for salvation is from the Jews. Yet a time is coming and has now come

Jesus: the life changer

when the true worshippers will worship the Father in spirit and truth, for they are the kind of worshippers the Father seeks. God is spirit, and his worshippers must worship in spirit and in truth.'

The woman said, 'I know that Messiah' (called Christ) 'is coming. When he comes, he will explain everything to us.'

Then Jesus declared, 'I who speak to you am he.' (John 4:1–26)

Think it through!

- What is unusual about Jesus' conversation with this woman?
- What does it tell us about the kind of people He came to reach?

- If you have ever thought that you were beyond God's help, how would this woman's encounter with Jesus challenge that assumption?

- How did Jesus use the water as an illustration of what He was communicating to this woman? Remember that they lived in a very arid climate.

- What did Jesus offer the Samaritan woman?

- Did Jesus come to establish a new religion? If not, what did He come for?

- What is Jesus talking about when He speaks of 'eternal life'? Is it something that you have?

6 Desperate measures

By **Asa Simeon***

Desperation can drive a cautious person to recklessness. Take me as an example! I have always considered myself to be a responsible person: I never act on impulse, I think before I do something, and I consider what the consequences might be. One day, however, my convictions got the better of my caution.

My friend Reuben was paralysed, and his life was utterly miserable. True, he had some good friends who took care of him; but from the moment he woke up to the second he drifted off to sleep, he had to struggle to do the most basic tasks—things you and I take for granted. Four of us took turns to help him wash, dress and eat. One day, we got together for a meal and started to talk about what else could be done for him. None of us could offer any new ideas but, just as we were about to go our separate ways, one of my friends suggested taking him to a 'healer'. I assumed he was talking about a doctor. The ones we had already seen were no help at all; they only deepened our gloom. 'We've tried that, and you know what they were like,' I said angrily. 'They took our money and shattered our hope. We can't go back to them!' My friend smiled and shook his head. 'That's not what I mean; the person I'm talking about is not a doctor. I want to take Reuben to the man everybody has been talking about—the one who has been travelling around, telling people about God and teaching them how to live differently.' I couldn't quite believe what I was hearing. 'Are you suggesting that we take him to a religious teacher? What is he going to do, teach him how to live with his paralysis?'

'No, you don't understand what I'm saying. Haven't you heard about Jesus' miracles?'

I sat upright in my chair. 'Let's give it a go,' I said. 'How do we find him?'

'That's the tricky part. Jesus travels around, so we'll need to keep our ears open and be ready to take Reuben to him as soon as we hear that he is near us.'

A few weeks later, I was at work when I spotted one of my friends running towards me. A rush of excitement surged through me as I realized why he looked so ecstatic. He gave me the news as soon as I was in shouting range: 'The man we were talking about is in town. Let's go and get Reuben!' Our other two friends were waiting for us, having heard the news themselves. One of them described it as our 'last hope', but the other said it was our 'best chance'. It is usually left to me to consider the practicalities. 'One little matter we haven't talked about yet,' I said calmly. 'How are we going to get him there?' Everyone looked around the room, and then one of my friends pointed to a mat. 'We'll lay him on there and carry him to where Jesus is. We don't have to go far—it's just a few streets down.'

> **One of them described it as our 'last hope', but the other said it was our 'best chance'. It is usually left to me to consider the practicalities.**

I have fought my way through the throngs of people who have come to the capital for a festival, but I have never seen crowds as dense as these or known an atmosphere as frenzied as this was. By the time we had arrived, Jesus looked like a small speck in the house he was speaking from. We stood and listened to his teaching; it was so different from the dull tone of the religious leaders I was used to. Jesus spoke of something he called 'God's Kingdom' and he told us that we could be part of it if we 'changed direction' and believed in him. It was totally new for me; religion always seemed dry and dusty, but Jesus seemed to be talking about something radically different, something that changed your life. He may have been difficult to see in the distance, I may have had to strain to hear him, but I was certain that he could help our friend as nobody had been able to before.

After Jesus finished, we tried to get through the crowd, but it was impossible, especially for four men carrying someone on a mat. 'What are we going to do now?' asked one of my friends with an air of desperation. Then I became uncharacteristically reckless. I noticed that the roof was made from clay and that some of us had knives. 'I've got it!' I said. 'We'll go round to the back of the house, climb onto the roof, dig a hole with our knives and lower Reuben into the house. Jesus won't be able to miss him then.' For a moment, the others looked at me with their mouths wide open. 'Come on!' I urged them. 'It's our only chance.'

The house Jesus had been visiting was small, with a flat roof which was made out of beams that went from one wall to another. We had all climbed onto the roofs of our own houses, so we were able to clamber up onto this one in no time at all. There was enough space between the beams to lower our friend down, so all that was left for us to do was to cut through the twigs, which were held together with clay. Our knives sliced through in an instant, then we attached the mat which carried our friend to some rope, carefully hauled it up onto the roof and lowered it through the hole we had made, waiting for Jesus' reaction.

I thought I had prepared myself for every eventuality, trying to anticipate what he might say and how he would react, but he did the last thing I expected.

I thought I had prepared myself for every eventuality, trying to anticipate what he might say and how he would react, but he did the last thing I expected. He turned around, looked at our friend and said. 'Take heart, my son, your sins are forgiven.'

This troubled me. Couldn't he see my friend's need? He hadn't come to be forgiven—he'd come to be healed! Perhaps Jesus thought Reuben was paralysed because he'd done something wicked. And that didn't seem to make sense; I know that Reuben wasn't perfect, but he'd never done anything to deserve this!

Some religious leaders were standing at the edge of the crowd and they had been listening to Jesus very carefully. They didn't like what he had been saying. I could imagine what was going through their minds: 'Who does he think he is? He insults God—he's the only one who can forgive sins!' Jesus knew what they were thinking and he went on the offensive: 'Which is easier to say—your sins are forgiven, or get up, pick up your mat and walk? I'm going to prove that I have authority to forgive sins.' This was a bold statement. Anyone could say 'your sins are forgiven'—it couldn't be proved either way—but if he were to tell my friend to pick up his mat and walk, one of two things could happen. My friend could still be lying there and Jesus would have failed, or my friend could be healed. As I thought about this, I realized what Jesus was getting at. It is more difficult to say 'get up and walk'—it will either succeed or fail—so if Jesus was able to do what seemed to be the harder thing, we could not dispute his claim that he could forgive sins. As I was thinking this over, one of my friends jabbed me in the ribs. 'What does he mean?' he asked. I picked up a twig, held it in front of me, and with my other hand lifted a stone. 'If I can pick up this heavy stone, I will be able to carry that little twig. Jesus is saying that if he can make Reuben walk, it is proof that he can forgive people.' But we had to stop talking: something was happening. Jesus turned round, looked at Reuben and said, 'Get up, take your mat with you and go home. You are healed!' The crowd was transfixed, and the religious leaders looked nervous; every eye was on Reuben. And he didn't just get up: he jumped up and then pushed his way through the stunned crowd!

> **'Jesus is saying that if he can make Reuben walk, it is proof that he can forgive people.'**

After the exhilaration had died down, I began to give the events of that day a lot of thought. When we stood inside that house, I could not understand why Jesus seemed to ignore the obvious need and speak about forgiveness from sin. I thought about my own sin, the things I had done wrong which had built up a barrier between God and myself, and I realized the wonder of Jesus' words. He hadn't come just to teach us about God and to heal the sick: he came to pull down that barrier, to bring us forgiveness, so that we could be part of the 'Kingdom' he told us about. He wasn't ignoring my friend's condition at all; he was pointing out his deeper need, a need which he was able to meet.

Jesus: the life changer **41**

A few days later, when Jesus again entered Capernaum, the people heard that he had come home. So many were gathered that there was no room left, not even outside the door, and he preached the word to them. Some men came, bringing to him a paralytic, carried by four of them. Since they could not get him to Jesus because of the crowd, they made an opening in the roof above Jesus and, after digging through it, lowered the mat the paralysed man was lying on. When Jesus saw their faith, he said to the paralytic, 'Son, your sins are forgiven.'

Now some teachers of the law were sitting there, thinking to themselves, 'Why does this fellow talk like that? He's blaspheming! Who can forgive sins but God alone?'

Immediately Jesus knew in his spirit that this was what they were thinking in their hearts, and he said to them, 'Why are you thinking these things? Which is easier: to say to the paralytic, "Your sins are forgiven," or to say, "Get up, take your mat and walk"? But that you may know that the Son of Man has authority on earth to forgive sins …' He said to the paralytic, 'I tell you, get up, take your mat and go home.' He got up, took his mat and walked out in full view of them all. This amazed everyone and they praised God, saying, 'We have never seen anything like this!' (Mark 2:1–12)

Think it through!

➤ Think about the lengths to which these men went to bring their friend to Jesus. What does it tell us about them?

➤ Mark writes that, as they lowered the man down, 'Jesus saw their faith'. What does he mean?

➤ What does this tell us about faith?

➤ Homight it help you to have faith?

➤ Why did Jesus tell the paralysed man that his sins were forgiven when he was brought to Him for healing?

➤ The religious leaders were thinking, 'Why does this fellow talk like that? He's blaspheming! Who can forgive sins but God alone?' What were they refusing to face up to?

➤ How does Jesus relate the healing of the paralysed man to His authority to forgive sins? What significance does this give to the miracle?

➤ What does this tell us about our deepest need? Has it been met in your life?

7 Lost and found

By **Zacchaeus of Jericho**

Have you ever wondered what the world would be like had you never existed? You can probably take comfort from the fact that things would have been different without you. Children would never have been born, parents wouldn't have been cared for in their old age or achievements wouldn't have been made. Most of us matter to someone. That's what made me different; I have wondered whether, had I never been born, the world might be a slightly better place!

To be honest, this is a problem of my own making. I have a job which has made me one of the most despised people around—I collect taxes, and people have good reason to hate me. For a start, nobody likes to part with their hard-earned money to pay taxes, but the real problem is that I have chosen to work for people who have invaded and occupied our land. It seemed such an attractive offer: I would be given a region to work in, be told the amount of money I had to pass on to the authorities, and then be allowed to charge as much as I wanted, keeping the excess for myself. This has made me very rich, but loneliness and isolation made it all seem so empty.

My employers saw that I was very good at my job and promoted me, sending me to work in a city that lay in the middle of a major trading route. This brought more money.

> **My success was fleeting and futile; it brought me everything I ever dreamed of, but the dream turned sour.**

However, the more affluent I became, the hollower it seemed. My success was fleeting and futile; it brought me everything I ever dreamed of, but the dream turned sour. During the long evenings I spent surrounded by luxury

44 Jesus: the life changer

and starved of human company, I sat and thought about how empty and worthless my life had become. And then I met someone who changed my life.

I was sitting at my table, enduring the usual hard looks and ignoring sarcastic comments made by people as they parted with their money. Business was unusually quiet, which gave me time to take in some of the sights, sounds and smells of the city. Nomads from the lands which lie in the east were majestically riding through the city gates on their camels and gazing into the distance. Clusters of tourists, bubbling with excitement, were pouring in, the young street traders running behind in the hope of selling something. There was an intriguing smell of different spices which had blended in the air, a hum of conversation and the chink of coins being exchanged as people did business.

Then a man purposefully swept into the city, with a mass of people trying to keep up with him. He walked down the main street, the crowd growing by the second. I knew many of these people, and the effect of this man's arrival on them was unbelievable. Traders dropped their goods and ran over to join the ever-expanding crowd. The young street peddlers broke off from their pursuit of the travellers, and people ran towards the man shouting, 'Teacher, teacher.' The noise was unlike anything I had ever heard before; it was as if one of the great Prophets had broken out of his grave to visit our city.

> **I knew many of these people, and the effect of this man's arrival on them was unbelievable.**

Everyone was running in this man's direction, so it was difficult to stop someone to find out what was going on. Eventually, I managed to grab the sleeve of a young boy. He tugged to get away from me, but I wouldn't let him go until he answered my question. 'It's Jesus,' he shouted, trying to overcome the noise of the crowd, 'the teacher and miracle-worker.' As I let go of his sleeve, he seemed to catapult into the crowd and push his way towards Jesus.

Suddenly, I became aware of my emptiness and realized that I needed to hear what Jesus had to say. But the crowd was huge and I was short; how could I get near him? I knew every inch of the city and remembered that a huge tree stood just beyond where he was heading. I ran to it and did something I thought I had left behind in my childhood—I climbed it!

Most people were too interested in Jesus to notice what I had done, although I could see one or two glance

Jesus: the life changer

up at me and shoot a filthy look in my direction. I was used to that, but then Jesus himself looked up. I felt the blood drain from me; what would he do? Would he reject me because of my profession? Would he call me a traitor? The very first thing he said made me think the worst—he called out my name, which meant he knew who I was and what I did for a living. But this pang of anxiety quickly dissolved. 'Come down immediately,' he said. 'I'm going to be a guest in your house today.' It was one of those moments when you cannot quite believe what is happening. Could he really be talking to me, the man people hated? Was he really going to give me the honour of providing him with hospitality? I could not quite believe it, but I scrambled down from the tree and stood next to him. There were mutterings coming from the crowd, and it wasn't too difficult to pick out what people were saying. 'Why does Jesus want to go to the house of such a rotten person? Doesn't he realize that he's a lost cause?' I didn't care what they thought; I knew this was going to be a turning point for me. Jesus was no ordinary teacher—he was able to bring God into people's lives, and he had told the crowd that, if this was going to happen to them, they needed to change their whole outlook on life. And that was just what I was going to do. I was going to put my greed, selfishness and dishonesty behind and live a new life. 'Look, Lord,' I said resolutely, 'I'm going to give half my possessions to the poor, and I'll repay anyone I have overcharged four times over!' I wasn't trying to get Jesus to accept me—I felt that he had already done so the moment he looked up and called my name. He had changed my life, forgiven me for my terrible deeds, freed me from the greed that enslaved me, and given my life a new direction. Jesus seemed to know this was my intention; he looked at me, turned to the crowd and said, 'Today salvation has come to this house, for I have come to seek out and restore people who are lost.'

For years, I did not matter; I was just another greedy, corrupt tax collector. The people saw me as a traitor; the religious leaders, as a hopeless case. But Jesus knew I was lost and came to find me.

JESUS entered Jericho and was passing through. A man was there by the name of Zacchaeus; he was a chief tax collector and was wealthy. He wanted to see who Jesus was, but being a short man he could not, because of the crowd. So he ran ahead and climbed a sycamore-fig tree to see him, since Jesus was coming that way.

When Jesus reached the spot, he looked up and said to him, 'Zacchaeus, come down immediately. I must stay at your house today.' So he came down at once and welcomed him gladly.

All the people saw this and began to mutter, 'He has gone to be the guest of a "sinner."'

But Zacchaeus stood up and said to the Lord, 'Look, Lord! Here and now I give half of my possessions to the poor, and if I have cheated anybody out of anything, I will pay back four times the amount.'

Jesus said to him, 'Today salvation has come to this house, because this man, too, is a son of Abraham. For the Son of Man came to seek and to save what was lost.' (Luke 19:1–10)

Think it through!

➤ What does Jesus' response to Zacchaeus tell us about His attitude to people and His love for them? Think about this in the context of the crowd's reaction to Jesus' request to eat with Zacchaeus.

MORE STUDY QUESTIONS ➤

- Why was Zacchaeus such an unpopular person?

- How does the crowd's reaction contrast with Zacchaeus' response to Jesus? Which response is most like yours?

- Who did Jesus come to 'seek and save'? Where does that leave you?

8 A shepherd in the wilderness

By **Philip of Bethsaida**

I was exhausted but elated. I had spent many days travelling from town to town, spreading a message Jesus had given me and healing people in his name. I longed to rest my weary bones and find solitude away from the hordes of people I had met on my travels. I wondered how Jesus had been able to keep up the pace for the last few years. He must have incredible drive, compassion and commitment to his mission. But although my body ached with tiredness and my head throbbed from the conversations and encounters I'd had over the last few days, I was full of excitement about what had been happening. Finally, my journey was over and my task complete. I was looking forward to seeing Jesus again and telling him everything that had happened.

I had travelled with Jesus, helped him, listened to him enthral the crowds with his teaching and watched the way he helped people—it was remarkable. The crowds that gathered around him stretched as far as the eye could see, but Jesus treated them as individuals, listening to their problems, answering their questions and healing their diseases. The other disciples and I observed, learned, and expressed our amazement to one another as we saw his enormous appeal, immense power and sensitive compassion. We were so different from him—we couldn't draw a crowd, heal people's sicknesses or show the degree of compassion Jesus had. In fact, we were a complete contrast to him—we were powerless, flawed, and impatient with people. And this often filled us with a sense of shame.

> **We were a complete contrast to him—we were powerless, flawed, and impatient with people.**

Then Jesus gave his surprising

announcement. He divided the twelve of us into pairs, gave us instructions and sent us out to do the kinds of things we had seen him do. We were to tell people to turn to God, drive out demons and heal the sick in his name. It took a moment for me to realize what he was telling us to do. I felt like stopping him and saying, 'Lord, are you sure this is right? Do you really think we can do this?' Then I thought about the practicalities—where would we stay, what would we eat, when were we going to gather what we needed for the journey? But Jesus had already thought about these things. 'All you need to take with you is your staff. You'll need no bread, no bag, no money.' He told us that in every town there would be people prepared to give us somewhere to sleep and something to eat. But not everyone would be helpful and hospitable—we would meet some who wouldn't want us to cross the boundary of their town, and we were to walk away from them, shaking the dust off our feet as a warning.

I was in the last few yards of my journey and I could see Jesus, surrounded by the other followers. The atmosphere was animated, and the noise of those men telling their news all at once echoed along the road I was walking on. Jesus looked so pleased, like a father who had watched his son take his first few steps. But his pleasure seemed to be tinged by sadness; he looked as though he had been weeping. Later, we found out that Herod had murdered Jesus' cousin John (the man who had preached in the desert and immersed people in water). News of our travels had disturbed Herod so much that he was trying to meet with Jesus and question him. All of this happened in one day, yet Jesus was undaunted.

Jesus looked so pleased, like a father who had watched his son take his first few steps.

All twelve of us were pouring out our news to Jesus.

'It's amazing, Lord—people turned from their sins and were healed of their sicknesses.'

'On the very first night we were wondering where we would stay when a man opened his door and welcomed us into his home. He said, "Any friend of Jesus is a friend of mine!" He gave us a room to sleep in, and his wife cooked us a meal, washed our dirty clothes and sent us away with food for our journey. They wouldn't hear of it when we thanked them for all they had done. "It's a pleasure to serve God in this way," they told us.'

'Lord, you were right when you

warned us that not everyone would welcome us with open arms. Some people wouldn't let us set foot in their town and threatened us, but we remembered that there were those who rejected you. So why should we be treated any differently?'

Jesus listened to our stories patiently. Eventually, he held up his hands to signal that we had said enough. 'Let's go to a place in the wilderness where we can get some rest,' he said.[9] I was surprised at this. We were tired and hungry, we had gone out in trepidation, done what he'd told us to do and come back with confidence. Why take us to a wilderness? Why not a lush oasis or a comfortable inn? But at least it would be a quiet place, away from the crowds and where we could relax.

The nearer we got to our destination, the deeper my heart sank. Some people who had been watching us gather around Jesus had followed us, and others who saw us as we passed through their villages swelled their number; eventually, they rushed past and arrived ahead of us. The wilderness wasn't the quiet place of solitude we had expected. I was tired of people and their problems; I wanted us to have some time to ourselves. I expected Jesus to send them away and tell them to come back another day. I was frustrated, irritated, tired and angry—but Jesus was so different. It struck me that, although we had completed the mission he had sent us on and were filled with a new sense of confidence, we were still a pale shadow of Jesus. We were weary of people, while he was welcoming; we wanted to send them away, while he wanted to teach them; we wanted to please ourselves, while he wanted to serve others.

> **If anyone had a right to say 'enough is enough' and refuse to help them, it was Jesus.**

If anyone had a right to say 'enough is enough' and refuse to help them, it was Jesus. He had heard that his cousin had suffered a hideous death, he had been told that Herod was seeking him out, and he had listened patiently to our excited reports. Although he was so different from us, he was still a real human being and he would have been coping with a mixture of emotions and reactions. He would have been longing to have some solitude and spend time with his friends, and his personal space was being invaded as much as ours. But he reacted differently.

We still reflect on that event and talk about the enormity of his compassion. Jesus regarded that crowd as 'sheep without a shepherd'.[10] They were noisy and confused, with no one to lead them. They were lost in life, desperate for a morsel of truth, and Jesus gave them what they needed: he taught them about God.

It was a familiar scene by now—crowds massing around Jesus, straining to hear his every word. I have never seen anyone hold a crowd's attention as he could. They didn't notice the air getting cooler or the sun going down until he had finished speaking to them.

Jesus had hardly uttered his last word when we came up to him with a suggestion. 'It's late in the day,' we told him. 'We haven't eaten and the crowd must be hungry. Why don't you send them away to the towns around here so that they can buy some food?' If I'm honest, I have to say that we weren't interested in their welfare at all—we just wanted some time to ourselves. But Jesus seemed to see right through our suggestion. He looked down for a moment, nodded his head knowingly, and then looked round us in a way that made us feel very uncomfortable. And he surprised us again! 'That's not really necessary—you give them something to eat.' I couldn't quite believe what I had heard. There were thousands of people milling around us. Where were we supposed to find enough food? And how could we afford to pay for it? 'But, Lord,' we protested, 'we'd need to work for eight months just to earn enough money to buy the bread.' But Jesus wasn't going to let it rest. He asked us to go out into the crowd and see how much food we could gather. We could only muster five small loaves and two fish that a boy had brought with him, but Jesus was happy with this.

He told us to get everyone to sit down in small groups; then he took the few loaves and fish we had given him, looked up to heaven in prayer, and began to divide up the food. It seemed to take a long time; I would have thought that those few loaves and fishes could have been broken up quickly, but it seemed to go on and on and on, producing more and more food—enough to feed the huge crowd. Afterwards, we gathered up twelve baskets of leftovers. The crowd had been fed, and there was still more to go round!

In the previous few days, I had seen the sick healed, demons driven out of people, lame people walking, deaf people hearing and blind people having their sight restored. I had set out nervously and come back full of confidence. I had been able to do the kinds of things Jesus had been doing. However, as I looked at the crowd—like a flock of sheep with no shepherd, lost, hungry and hurting—and saw how Jesus cared for them, I realized all the more how much greater he was.

THE apostles gathered round Jesus and reported to him all they had done and taught. Then, because so many people were coming and going that they did not even have a chance to eat, he said to them, 'Come with me by yourselves to a quiet place and get some rest.'

So they went away by themselves in a boat to a solitary place. But many who saw them leaving recognised them and ran on foot from all the towns and got there ahead of them. When Jesus landed and saw a large crowd, he had compassion on them, because they were like sheep without a shepherd. So he began teaching them many things.

By this time it was late in the day, so his disciples came to him. 'This is a remote place,' they said, 'and it's already very late. Send the people away so that they can go to the surrounding countryside and villages and buy themselves something to eat.'

But he answered, 'You give them something to eat.'

They said to him, 'That would take eight months of a man's wages! Are we to go and spend that much on bread and give it to them to eat?'

'How many loaves do you have?' he asked. 'Go and see.'

When they found out, they said, 'Five—and two fish.'

Then Jesus directed them to have all the people sit down in groups on the green grass. So they sat down in groups of hundreds and fifties. Taking the five loaves and the two fish and looking up to heaven, he gave thanks and broke the loaves. Then he gave them to his disciples to set before the people. He also divided the two fish among them all. They all ate and were satisfied, and the disciples picked up twelve basketfuls of broken pieces of bread and fish. The number of the men who had eaten was five thousand.
(Mark 6:30–44)

Think it through!

➢ What was the original intention of Jesus and the disciples' visit to the 'remote place'?

➢ How does Jesus' attitude towards the crowds contrast with that of the disciples?

➢ Read the following passages from the Old Testament:

> The Lord is my shepherd, I shall not be in want. He makes me lie down in green pastures, he leads me beside quiet waters, he restores my soul. He guides me in paths of righteousness for his name's sake. Even though I walk through the valley of the shadow of death, I will fear no evil, for you are with me; your rod and your staff, they comfort me. You prepare a table before me in the presence of my enemies. You anoint my head with oil; my cup overflows. Surely goodness and love will follow me all the days of my life, and I will dwell in the house of the Lord for ever. (Psalm 23)

> For this is what the Sovereign Lord says: I myself will search for my sheep and look after them. As a shepherd looks after his scattered flock when he is with them, so will I look after my sheep. I will rescue them from all the places where they were scattered on a day of clouds and darkness. I will bring them out from the nations and gather them from the countries, and I will bring them into their own land. I will pasture them on the mountains of Israel, in the ravines and in all the settlements in the land. I will tend them in a good pasture, and the mountain heights of Israel will be their grazing land. There they will lie down in good grazing land, and there they will feed in a rich pasture on the mountains of Israel. I myself will tend my sheep and make them lie down, declares the Sovereign Lord. I will search for the lost and bring back the strays. I will bind up the injured and strengthen the weak, but the sleek and the strong I will destroy. I will shepherd the flock with justice. (Ezekiel 34:11–16)

➢ How do these verses help us understand Mark's statement that Jesus had compassion on the crowd 'because they were like sheep without a shepherd'?

9 A traveller's tale

By **Isaac of Gedara***

Another day, another town, another opportunity to tell my story; and although I have already told it to many people, I could repeat it a thousand times more. I like to watch their reactions as I speak—terror as I relay the grim details of my old life, relief when I tell them how it all changed, and wonder at the power of the one who brought about such a transformation. The sun is climbing into the sky, the heat is rising, and I should be moving on to seek another crowd before the midday heat drives them off the streets. But if you could spare me the time, I would like to tell this great story to you.

I expect you got up this morning, did the same things you had done the day before and thought nothing of it. It isn't like that for me. I find an incredible joy in the ordinary routines of life—getting out of bed after a good night's sleep, opening the blinds to let the sun dispel the darkness, eating breakfast and greeting my neighbours. Until recently, these simple things were impossible for me because I lived like an animal, sleeping in the caves and scavenging for scraps of food. I can't really remember when or how it all started, but at the beginning of my ordeal, people seemed to be amused. Youths would stand outside the cave shouting abuse and taunting me. Boats on the lake would stop and people would point to me. Then they decided that I was a danger to them. The biggest, strongest men in the town marched up to the cave, seized me and chained me up. 'That will help people to sleep more soundly at night,' they said. I was seething with anger, bellowing threats and screaming at the top of my voice. I pulled at the chains and snapped them as easily as I would have broken a twig. Was this a stroke of luck, or had my strength multiplied? I did the same thing with the shackles they had put around my hands and feet, tearing them away and smashing them on the rocks. 'Look at my strength!' I roared. 'You'll never be able to control me!'

From then on, nobody came near the caves. People from my town will tell you that I could be seen wandering the hillside, smashing myself with stones and rocks. My blood-curdling screams could be heard for miles around.

If you have ever had a terrible nightmare that you couldn't wake up from, you'll have some idea of what my life had become. I sensed another power seizing my body, making me do the most dreadful things and filling me with terror in the process. It was no longer my life—it belonged to whatever had taken control of me. You couldn't imagine a more sinister place than those caves. They were used to bury dead bodies and they reeked of death and decay, but the evil power that controlled me seemed to revel in the atmosphere and used it to terrify the locals.

Another atrocious night had come to an end and the prospect of another desperate day arrived, when I noticed a boat landing on the shore. Thirteen men got out and one of them, who was obviously the leader, pointed to where I was. I wondered who this could be. It's difficult to explain, but from the moment I set eyes on the man, two contrasting things happened within me: a sense of hope reawakened the part of me that existed before this power had taken hold of me, and the evil power itself was gripped with terror. Despite this, it pushed me towards the man so forcefully that I ran to meet him. It was as if the visitor had summoned me into his presence and the evil power had no choice in the matter. Still under its control, I screamed, spat and shouted at the man.

I had never set eyes on this man before, but this evil power within me knew him well.

First came the hate-filled greeting, as if an old enemy had come to speak to me: 'What do you want with me, Jesus, Son of the Most High God?' I had never set eyes on this man before, but this evil power within me knew him well. I had spoken with such venom and malice that any other person would have turned and run, but this man was different. He stayed where he was, looked me in the eye and spoke directly to the evil power: 'Come out of the man, you evil spirit!' And suddenly I realized what had been living inside me, desecrating my life and terrifying everyone who came into contact with me. The evil spirit was petrified and it began to plead with the man: 'Swear to me, Jesus, Son of God, that you won't torture me.' It seemed as if Judgement

Day had come early: as if this evil spirit had been dragged into God's presence, embodied in this man Jesus, and seen its own doom. Jesus demanded to know the name of the evil spirit. 'My name is Legion,' it made me say, 'for we are many.' It was as if I was standing by, watching and realizing what had been happening to me for all this time. I had been possessed by a host of evil spirits calling themselves 'Legion'. The name spoke of enormity, oppression and strength. It reminded me of the Roman soldiers who forced their iron will on our country and visited any trace of rebellion with brute force.

How ironic that this formidable mass of evil spirits was stripped of power by one man! Again and again, they pleaded with Jesus not to be sent away, and eventually asked him to send them into a herd of pigs on a nearby hill. They had gripped my life and rendered my own will powerless, but now they couldn't even take possession of a herd of animals without Jesus allowing them to.

The first thing I was aware of was the ear-piercing squeal of a herd of pigs.

The ordeal came to a sudden, liberating end. I was free, in control and alert. I was myself again! The first thing I was aware of was the ear-piercing squeal of a herd of pigs and the thud of their feet on the ground as they ran towards the cliff and fell to their deaths. Jesus had allowed the evil spirits to go into the pigs, and their very last act was one of wanton destruction. He looked at me in a way that suggested he knew everything about the agony I had endured. He must have come there just to free me. This man who could inspire fear in a mass of evil spirits and restore a life as desperate as mine amazed me. I looked at him, opened my mouth and stuttered a few words, lifting up my arms to help me express my astonishment and delight. 'Jesus, please let me travel with you, learn about you and help you,' I begged. He looked at me, and his face reflected a sense of authority. 'That's not what I want you to do,' he said gently. 'I want you to go home to your friends and tell them about the wonderful things the Lord has done for you, and how merciful he has been to you.'

And that's why I am here, telling you my story.

THEY sailed to the region of the Gerasenes, which is across the lake from Galilee. When Jesus stepped ashore, he was met by a demon-possessed man from the town. For a long time this man had not worn clothes or lived in a house, but had lived in the tombs. When he saw Jesus, he cried out and fell at his feet, shouting at the top of his voice, 'What do you want with me, Jesus, Son of the Most High God? I beg you, don't torture me!' For Jesus had commanded the evil spirit to come out of the man. Many times it had seized him, and though he was chained hand and foot and kept under guard, he had broken his chains and had been driven by the demon into solitary places.

Jesus asked him, 'What is your name?'

'Legion,' he replied, because many demons had gone into him. And they begged him repeatedly not to order them to go into the Abyss.

A large herd of pigs was feeding there on the hillside. The demons begged Jesus to let them go into them, and he gave them permission. When the demons came out of the man, they went into the pigs, and the herd rushed down the steep bank into the lake and was drowned.

When those tending the pigs saw what had happened, they ran off and reported this in the town and countryside, and the people went out to see what had happened. When they came to Jesus, they found the man from whom the demons had gone out, sitting at Jesus' feet, dressed and in his right mind; and they were afraid. Those who had seen it told the people how the demon-possessed man had been cured. Then all the people of the region of the Gerasenes asked Jesus to leave them, because they were overcome with fear. So he got into the boat and left.

The man from whom the demons had gone out begged to go with him, but Jesus sent him away, saying, 'Return home and tell how much God has done for you.' So the man went away and told all over the town how much Jesus had done for him. (Luke 8:26–39)

Think it through!

➢ What does the evil spirits' reaction to Jesus tell us about His authority?

➢ Describe the change that Jesus brought about in this man's life.

MORE STUDY QUESTIONS ▶

Jesus: the life changer

> What did Jesus want the man to do? How would this extend His authority?

> Colossians 2:15 says that, 'having disarmed the powers and authorities, [Jesus] made a public spectacle of them, triumphing over them by the cross'. How does the incident you have just read about foreshadow this?

10 The King breaks in

By **Salome Terassa***

Children constantly change; they develop, learn and quickly adapt to the challenges of life. However, my daughter's change was different. At first, I thought nothing of the aggression and the strange way in which she sometimes spoke to me; but as the dark moods multiplied and the violent behaviour intensified, I realized that something was seriously wrong. A little later, I was told that she was possessed by a demon and that nothing could be done for her. In the weeks that followed, she withdrew into her own private world and often broke out in fits of violence.

Everyone was talking about a man called Jesus and I began to wonder if he might be the only person who could help my daughter, even though I was not one of his own people. The Jews drew great comfort from promises in their Scriptures; unlike us, they worshipped one who they said was the only true God, 'the maker of heaven and earth'. He was all-powerful, and throughout their history he had done incredible things to rescue and help them. They were now ruled by the Romans but they drew hope from a promise in their Scriptures that God would bring them a King who would be a son of David—the greatest ruler in their history. He would rescue them from their enemies and rule over them in justice. Could Jesus be the one they were anticipating?

> **I began to wonder if he might be the only person who could help my daughter, even though I was not one of his own people.**

Jesus had come to our region to rest, and I decided to look for him and beg for his help.

I found him sitting quietly, deep in thought, and I suddenly broke into tears. Jesus was looking at me, and those striking eyes seemed to pierce right into my soul. He provoked a mixture of emotions and reactions in me: a sense of fear, but different from the kind my daughter often evoked in me when she flew into one of her fits and cursed me. This was a realization that I was in the presence of someone who was truly great. I tried to fight back my tears, struggling to get my words out: 'Have mercy on me, Lord, Son of David! My daughter is demon-possessed!'

He provoked a mixture of emotions and reactions in me.

My heart was pounding as I waited for his answer, but he was silent, completely silent. This man who had told enthralling stories, made impassioned speeches and taught people his radical ideas with such authority didn't say a word to me. I stood in front of him, determined not to move until he gave me an answer—he was my only hope. The tension was suddenly broken by the arrival of some other men, who were his followers. There wasn't the deep compassion in their eyes that I had seen in Jesus'. 'Master, we came here for a rest,' one of them protested. 'Can't you send this woman away so that we can have some peace and quiet?' Jesus' eyes were locked onto mine as he said, 'I was sent only to the lost sheep of the house of Israel.' I dropped to my knees and, through deep sobs, I said, 'Lord, help me.' His words seemed hard, but the tone of his voice was still full of compassion and kindness. 'It is not right to take the children's bread and throw it to the dogs,' he said. His people often look down on us and call us 'dogs', but Jesus used the word in a different way: it seemed to be a challenge rather than a rejection, and I responded to it. 'But Lord, even the dogs eat the crumbs that fall from their master's table.' I could only plead for his mercy, and I was prepared to be considered the lowest person imaginable if only he could cure my daughter.

I was prepared to be considered the lowest person imaginable if only he could cure my daughter.

This was my last chance. The conversation was about to be closed and Jesus was ready to move on. Was I deluded to think that I could place myself under the rule of this new King? Then the strained silence was broken and his expression changed as he said, 'Your faith is great! I will give you what you want.' Then he put his hand on my shoulder, and left.

I made my way home with my mind reeling. What had he meant, and why

Jesus: the life changer **63**

didn't he come to see my daughter? I gently opened the door of our little house with my heart pounding. My little girl was sitting up; she smiled at me, spoke to me, and told me that a little while ago she felt as if she had just woken up from a terrible nightmare. Jesus' power had broken into our lives. Now he was our King, too.

LEAVING that place, Jesus withdrew to the region of Tyre and Sidon. A Canaanite woman from that vicinity came to him, crying out, 'Lord, Son of David, have mercy on me! My daughter is suffering terribly from demon-possession.'

Jesus did not answer a word. So his disciples came to him and urged him, 'Send her away, for she keeps crying out after us.'

He answered, 'I was sent only to the lost sheep of Israel.'

The woman came and knelt before him. 'Lord, help me!' she said.

He replied, 'It is not right to take the children's bread and toss it to their dogs.'

'Yes, Lord,' she said, 'but even the dogs eat the crumbs that fall from their masters' table.'

Then Jesus answered, 'Woman, you have great faith! Your request is granted.' And her daughter was healed from that very hour. (Matthew 15:21–28)

Think it through!

➤ What difference does this woman's nationality make to her approach to Jesus?

➤ Why did Jesus say that he was only sent 'to the lost sheep of Israel'? Look at Isaiah 53:6 and Ezekiel 34:10–16 to understand the background to his words.

Jesus: the life changer

➢ Think about the responses the woman made to Jesus: 'Lord, help me!' and 'Yes, Lord, but even the dogs eat the crumbs that fall from their masters' table'. What do they tell us about faith?

➢ What hope does this woman's experience give to you?

➢ How does her experience help us to have faith in Jesus and approach him?

11 A conflict in the crypt

By **various witnesses**

The doorman

Most of my friends spend their days shut away in workshops. They tell me how confined it makes them feel, and how they long for their days off so that they can enjoy the open space of the countryside. Although they are paid more than me, I would never wish to swap places with them. Unlike my friends, I am 'unskilled'; my job is to stand at the door of a building, be ready to help anyone who has a question or a problem, and stop 'undesirables' from coming in. It may not sound very interesting, but I enjoy every minute of it, and I go home each day feeling that I have done something valuable, because I am Temple doorkeeper.

Every day, I leave home, look up and see the magnificent building dominating the landscape: the four turrets looking out onto the city, the gold on the portico, blazing in the sun, and the formidable walls, wrapping themselves around it. Who could imagine a more elegant place to spend each day? I am privileged to work here! Although my job description is quite brief, I do not take my duties lightly because I have been entrusted with great responsibility. I am the first personal contact people have with the Temple, and the help I am able to give them can make all the difference to their visit. It is also very important for me to look out for any sign of trouble which may disrupt what is going on inside, so that people's worship is not disturbed.

The Temple has become a very noisy place. When I started working there, traders and moneychangers were given permission to set up stalls outside the building. At first, just a handful of them came, and they gave a valuable service to people who had travelled a distance. Some needed to change currency in order to put money in the offering, others needed livestock to offer as sacrifices, and they were very glad to be able to get what they needed. Gradually, more and more gathered outside and eventually they caused so much confusion that the authorities decided to let them set up their stalls in the outer court. This drew even more of them, and now it is more like a market than a temple! All I hear is the bleating of sheep, the bellowing of calves, the chink of money, and the shout of traders offering their services.

That takes me to the man who had the courage to do something about it. He was not a Priest or religious leader, but he seemed to care deeply about the worship that went on in the Temple. I could tell that he was the kind of person who put God before anything else. I first noticed him when I spotted him on the horizon, striding towards me with a small group of people running to keep up with him.

I have never seen such an expression before; he looked angry, but his anger seemed to be completely under control.

He nodded at me as he passed through the doorway. I have never seen such an expression before; he looked angry, but his anger seemed to be completely under control. The noises coming from inside suddenly changed; I could hear a whip lashing, animals running, and loud thuds, as if something was falling to the ground. I ran through the door, wondering whether something had collapsed and caused the commotion, but this man seemed to be behind it. He had made a whip out of cords and used it to drive the animals away from the stalls, and then pushed the tables over. Once I got closer, I was able to hear what he was saying. He was angry about the trading going on; he said they had turned his 'father's house' into a market place. I haven't been able to get this out of my mind. Surely he couldn't be saying what it sounded as if he was saying! The Temple is a place where people go to present their sacrifices to God and to worship him—it is God's house, so when he called it his father's house, he was claiming to be God's Son! That would be an astounding claim to make! Madmen have made this kind of assertion before, but he was sane. Liars have said similar things in cynical attempts to exploit and manipulate people, but he was transparently honest. I can only conclude that he was telling the truth, which means that we must listen to what he says and do what he asks of us.

The official

My colleague is always quick to spot any sign of trouble. A few days ago, he pointed out a man surrounded by people who seemed to be hanging on his every word. 'They're doing no harm,' I said, 'leave them alone.' If I had done something then I wouldn't have to answer for the commotion that went on this morning.

The first I knew of it was when my colleague burst into my room and told me to go out into the courtyard. It looked like a battlefield! There were tables lying on the ground, animals scurrying around in every direction, and traders cowering in fear. It was the work of one man—the one pointed out to me the day before. I had never been happy with what went on in the courtyard so, initially, I was quite pleased this had happened. It reminded me of something written by one of our Prophets about a messenger who would come to the temple:

> Who can endure the day of his coming?
> Who can stand when he appears?[11]

Although I had some sympathy with his actions, it was my responsibility to challenge him. I asked him to do a miracle to prove that he had the authority to act in such a way. My sympathy evaporated when he answered me. He said that, if the temple were to be destroyed, he would put it back together in three days. What could he possibly be talking about? I looked at him with an expression that showed I wasn't going to take him seriously any more. 'Come on,' I said, 'look around you—this building took years to construct; how could you possibly demolish it and then rebuild in three days?' I turned away in contempt, furious at his threat and determined to do everything in my power to rid our people of this troublesome man.

A follower's reflection

Sometimes, life with Jesus seemed a little like a puzzle—we pieced together things that Jesus said, but we couldn't always understand everything he told us because an important part seemed to be missing.

> **I will never forget the way he stormed into the Temple and caused such a commotion. It seemed so different from the side of him we were familiar with.**

I am glad to say that it has now all come together; Jesus has died, and risen from the dead, and we can now look back on some of the things that happened in our years together in a new way. I will never forget the way he stormed into the Temple and caused such a commotion. It seemed so different from the side of him we were familiar with;

he was angry, although it was not the self-centred emotion that often wells up in me. He was angry for his Father's sake; and he was in complete control of himself.

I was baffled most of all by his answer to the official. I had seen him do miracles, but I couldn't even imagine a miracle like the one he spoke about! Did he really think he would pull the Temple down and rebuild it in the space of three days? But now I understand; he was talking about himself, not the building. The Temple was a place where people met with God and asked him to forgive their sins. When Jesus died, he did away with the sacrifices and prayers offered by the Priests on our behalf, forging a link between heaven and earth and himself becoming the means by which we meet God.

JESUS entered the temple area and drove out all who were buying and selling there. He overturned the tables of the money-changers and the benches of those selling doves. 'It is written,' he said to them, '"My house will be called a house of prayer", but you are making it a "den of robbers".'

The blind and the lame came to him at the temple, and he healed them. But when the chief priests and the teachers of the law saw the wonderful things he did and the children shouting in the temple area, 'Hosanna to the Son of David,' they were indignant.

'Do you hear what these children are saying?' they asked him.

'Yes,' replied Jesus, 'have you never read, "From the lips of children and infants you have ordained praise"?'

And he left them and went out of the city to Bethany, where he spent the night. (Matthew 21:12–17)

Think it through!

- Does it surprise you to read about Jesus being angry?
- What does this add to your understanding of Him?

Jesus: the life changer

➢ What was He angry about?

➢ What does this tell us about His principles and values?

➢ How did these principles and values set Jesus apart from the religious leaders of His day?

12 A view from the shadows

By **Judas Iscariot**

I have never been one to enthuse about a new idea or join the latest movement. I prefer to lurk in the shadows, watch what is happening and wait to see whether it shows signs of success before I commit myself to it.

For once, though, I broke with my normal practice. When Jesus came along, called me to leave my job and follow him, I surprised everyone, including myself, by doing what he asked. We had some great times, which convinced me that I had done the right thing. When Jesus first took us from village to village with his message about God's Kingdom, a huge movement seemed to spring up from nowhere. People clamoured to see him; they would travel great distances, go to extraordinary lengths and hang onto his every word. Remarkable things were happening; people came to him blind, deaf and lame, and went away seeing, hearing and walking. Demons were driven out of the most terrifying, violent people I had ever met, and others seemed to change their whole lifestyles after they had met Jesus. One day he sent us, his followers, out in pairs, telling us that we were going to do his work, and we saw the same kinds of miracles happen at our hands. They were certainly the golden days.

But then things began to change. Increasingly, we seemed to spend less time at those gatherings when the masses would come to meet Jesus, and more time alone with him. Then he told us that we would be going to Jerusalem. 'Now you're talking,' I thought to myself. 'There will be thousands of people eager to meet with Jesus in Jerusalem—it will be the most thrilling event yet!' But Jesus' mind was on death. He told us that, when he arrived in Jerusalem, he would be rejected by the religious leaders and killed. This wasn't what I had joined for! I wanted excitement, action and acclaim, not rejection and death. The sense of hope that Jesus awakened in me melted away in the face of my disappointment and cynicism.

The other disciples were still enthusiastic and idealistic. They vowed to be with Jesus whatever happened and listened intently to everything he told them, and I began to feel bitter towards them. I tried not to show it, but Jesus seemed to know exactly what I was thinking, which made it very difficult to be near him.

The sense of hope that Jesus awakened in me melted away in the face of my disappointment and cynicism.

After we had arrived in Jerusalem, we travelled to a village that lay just outside the city. A man called Simon had invited us to his home; Jesus had healed him from leprosy and he wanted to have the meal in his honour. Simon had arranged for Jesus' friends Mary and Martha to cook and serve the meal.

Jesus, the other disciples, Lazarus (the brother of Mary and Martha whom Jesus had raised from the dead) and I were reclining at the table. The meal began, conversation broke out, and then Mary appeared at Jesus' side holding a jar of very rare, expensive perfume. This was no surprise in itself, as it was the custom to put a few drops on an honoured guest, but Mary snapped the top off the bottle and drained the entire contents onto Jesus' head. The babble of conversation subsided as everyone looked at her with surprise. A familiar feeling of bitterness and scorn rose in my heart. 'What does that woman think she's doing?' I said indignantly. 'Doesn't she realize how expensive that stuff is?' The perfume she used would have been in the family for generations; her mother would have given it to her expecting her to pass it on to her own daughter, but Mary had squandered it all in a reckless act of devotion to Jesus. I began to mutter to the person sitting next to me. 'Just think what she could have done with that perfume,' I said. 'A bottle could have been sold for a whole year's worth of wages, and the money used to help the poor.' My reasoning seemed to strike a note with him and with the others who listened to what I said. Passover was coming up, and it was customary to give to the poor. I persuaded them that a gesture like that could have made a real difference. They nodded and started to speak about the kinds of projects the money could have been used for, not knowing the hatred that was seething within me. But as soon as Jesus looked at me, I felt as if my very soul was being scrutinized. 'Leave her alone,' he said. 'Why are you bothering her? She has done a beautiful thing to me.'[12] I looked away from Jesus' piercing eyes and saw Mary's cheeks flush with embarrassment. The other followers dropped their heads in shame and I felt completely out of place, especially when Jesus returned to the theme I had grown so tired of. 'You will always have the poor with you and you can help them any time you want. But I won't be here much longer. Mary has done what she can for me. She has anointed my body so that it is ready for burial.' Mary had always paid close attention when Jesus was speaking. Once, she was listening to him so carefully that she forgot to help her sister Martha prepare the food, but when Martha complained, Jesus commended what Mary had done: 'Mary has chosen the better thing,' he said. For some time, Jesus had been saying that he was going to die, and I have no doubt that Mary, his best listener, would have taken notice of this. But her response was so different from mine, and for a moment I felt ashamed. Peter had reacted to the news with bravado: 'I'll never let it happen!' he said. The others responded with confusion, I grew cynical and disillusioned, but Mary seemed to want to honour Jesus before his death.

I soon pushed these thoughts out of my mind and decided that I'd had enough, but I wanted to get something back from the three years I had invested in Jesus' cause. The opportunity came when I met some of his fiercest critics: religious leaders. They hated him so much that they wanted him dead, but they realized how popular he was and were frightened that, if they arrested him during the feast of the Passover, it might provoke a riot. 'If you want Jesus, I can give him into your hands when there is no crowd around him,' I said. They looked at one another with expressions of pleasure and bewilderment on their faces. One of them said, 'Why would you want to do that?' 'I've had enough of following him,' I replied. 'I want out, and if you'll make it worth my while, I'll give him into your hands.' They looked at one another again, and this time they looked overjoyed. 'You're on,' they said. 'Tell us where to find him and we'll pay you in silver.' At last, there was an end in sight; the deal was struck, the deed was done, and I was going to come out of it with something. I walked the winding road home thinking about Mary's little display of devotion and laughing to myself. I was the winner in all of this, and she was the loser. Jesus would soon be dead and the cause would be lost. Where would that leave her?

SIX days before the Passover, Jesus arrived at Bethany, where Lazarus lived, whom Jesus had raised from the dead. Here a dinner was given in Jesus' honour. Martha served, while Lazarus was among those reclining at the table with him. Then Mary took about a pint of pure nard, an expensive perfume; she poured it on Jesus' feet and wiped his feet with her hair. And the house was filled with the fragrance of the perfume.

But one of his disciples, Judas Iscariot, who was later to betray him, objected, 'Why wasn't this perfume sold and the money given to the poor? It was worth a year's wages.' He did not say this because he cared about the poor but because he was a thief; as keeper of the money bag, he used to help himself to what was put into it.

'Leave her alone,' Jesus replied. 'It was intended that she should save this perfume for the day of my burial. You will always have the poor among you, but you will not always have me.'

Meanwhile a large crowd of Jews found out that Jesus was there and came, not only because of him but also to see Lazarus, whom he had raised from the dead. So the chief priests made plans to kill Lazarus as well, for on account of him many of the Jews were going over to Jesus and putting their faith in him. (John 12:1–11)

Think it through!

➢ Why was Judas so critical of Mary?

➢ Why do you think the religious leaders wanted Jesus to be killed?

MORE STUDY QUESTIONS ▶

Jesus: the life changer

➢ Mark's Gospel gives us some extra details about their plot:

> Now the Passover and the Feast of Unleavened Bread were only two days away, and the chief priests and the teachers of the law were looking for some sly way to arrest Jesus and kill him. 'But not during the Feast,' they said, 'or the people may riot.' (Mark 14:1–2)

➢ What stood in the way of them carrying out their plan?

➢ How did Judas' offer change this?

➢ What did Jesus say about Mary's act of devotion to Him?

➢ How did he influence the other disciples? Do you think there is someone who might be influencing you to be cynical about people who are devoted to Jesus?

➢ Contrast Mary's attitude to that of Judas and the disciples. Which is most like your attitude?

13 A diary of my disappointment

By **Simon Peter**

It is the end of a turbulent day and the middle of a terrible night. Just a few yards away, Jesus stands on trial before the religious leaders. I came here to show him my support, but now I am desperately aware that I have let him down.

A little while ago, I was crouched by a fire in the temple courtyard, shivering, though more from fear than from cold. The sight of the flames dancing in the cold night air gave me a few moments' relief from this nightmare. But it was broken when a girl stopped to speak to me. 'Weren't you with that man who is on trial?' I wanted to show my loyalty to Jesus, but I lost my nerve and let him down: 'I don't know what you're talking about!' I snapped. And as I was speaking, I was faintly aware of the sound of a rooster crowing. I left the reassuring warmth of the fire and retreated to the entrance of the courtyard.

A few minutes later, I heard her talking about me. 'That man is definitely one of his followers,' she was saying.

'Please leave me alone, I'm not who you think I am,' I pleaded.

> **I came here to show him my support, but now I am desperately aware that I have let him down.**

They left me in peace and I breathed a heavy sigh of relief, which was swiftly followed by a stab of self-recrimination. Then another person came to speak to me, and my heart plummeted. 'You're from the north—you must be one of his followers.' Anger was simmering up inside me and I wanted to be left alone, so I swore at them and called down curses upon myself. 'Look, I don't know the man you are talking about!' I said with an air of exasperation. Then, for the second time, I heard a rooster crowing, and Jesus' words, 'You will deny me before the rooster crows twice', came into my mind.

Now I have completely abandoned my attempt to show some kind of frail support for Jesus and have found a lonely spot where I can sit, think and try to work out what is going on.

My mind goes back to the day when Jesus took us away from the crowds so that we could spend some time together. It was a beautiful place, so quiet, so peaceful and so restful after many hectic weeks of travelling. 'Who do people say that I am?' he asked. There were several theories going round, and we told Jesus about each of them. From the look on his face, I realized that he was asking this question for our benefit. 'Who do you say that I am?' he asked us.

I gave the answer, 'You are the King that God has promised to send us, the Son of the living God.' Jesus looked at me, smiled knowingly and said, 'You haven't worked this out for yourself—my Father in heaven has shown this to you.'

Jesus was a fascinating person to be with—you never knew where a conversation would lead, and this one took a very unexpected turn! He told us that we were going to travel up to Jerusalem, where he would suffer at the hands of the religious authorities and be put to death, and that three days later he was going to rise from the dead. I couldn't accept what he was saying. 'Never!' I protested. 'I won't let it happen!' I thought he might be touched by this display of loyalty, but I couldn't have been more wrong. I will never forget those chilling words:

'Get away from me Satan! You are a dangerous trap to me. You are seeing things merely from a human point of view, not from God's.'[13]

He was so convinced that it was right to go to Jerusalem to die that any attempt to talk him out of it was seen as playing his enemy's role.

I wondered who he was speaking to. Perhaps he just happened to be looking in my direction and was talking to an unseen enemy. But I soon realized that his words were directed at me. He was so convinced that it was right to go to Jerusalem to die that any attempt to talk him out of it was seen as playing his enemy's role. I tried not to think of those alarming predictions; instead, I focused on the hope we had invested in Jesus. He talked about his death on two other occasions, but the tumultuous reception he was given as he entered Jerusalem made me doubt whether anything would happen to him. As the week wore on, though, the atmosphere changed. The religious leaders, who had always opposed Jesus, became more aggressive in their attacks. Each day they tried to pick arguments with him, but they could never get the better of Jesus.

During our last meal with Jesus, he told us that one of us was going to betray him. Shortly after he said this, Judas, our fellow disciple, slipped out of the room to strike a bargain with the people who wanted Jesus killed; a few hours later, Jesus was arrested.

Now I am separated from my friends, and Jesus stands trial before his fiercest critics. How can he be the King God promised us, yet face such a humiliating end? What was the point of all those miracles and wonderful stories over the past three years? And what hope is there for someone who has let him down as badly as I have?

WHEN Jesus came to the region of Caesarea Philippi, he asked his disciples, 'Who do people say the Son of Man is?'

They replied, 'Some say John the Baptist; others say Elijah; and still others, Jeremiah or one of the prophets.'

'But what about you?' he asked. 'Who do you say I am?'

Simon Peter answered, 'You are the Christ, the Son of the living God.'

Jesus replied, 'Blessed are you, Simon son of Jonah, for this was not revealed to you by man, but by my Father in heaven. And I tell you that you are Peter, and on this rock I will build my church, and the gates of Hades will not overcome it. I will give you the keys of the kingdom of heaven; whatever you bind on earth will be bound in heaven, and whatever you loose on earth will be loosed in heaven.' Then he warned his disciples not to tell anyone that he was the Christ. (Matthew 16:13–20)

'This word "Christ" has big implications. It means "God's Anointed one"; it's a title of supreme authority, like "King". Peter is saying that Jesus is the ultimate King, the one promised in the Bible, the one who would rescue all those who trusted in Him.' (Rico Tice, *Christianity Explored* (Carlisle: Authentic Media, p. 104)

From that time on Jesus began to explain to his disciples that he must go to Jerusalem and suffer many things at the hands of the elders, chief priests and teachers of the law, and that he must be killed and on the third day be raised to life.

Peter took him aside and began to rebuke him. 'Never, Lord!' he said. 'This shall never happen to you!'

Jesus turned and said to Peter, 'Get behind me, Satan! You are a stumbling-block to me; you do not have in mind the things of God, but the things of men.' (Matthew 16:21–23)

'Simon, Simon, Satan has asked to sift you as wheat. But I have prayed for you, Simon, that your faith may not fail. And when you have turned back, strengthen your brothers.'

But he replied, 'Lord, I am ready to go with you to prison and to death.'

Jesus answered, 'I tell you, Peter, before the cock crows today, you will deny three times that you know me.' (Luke 22:31–34)

Then seizing him, they led him away and took him into the house of the high priest. Peter followed at a distance. But when they had kindled a fire in the middle of the courtyard and had sat down together, Peter sat down with them. A servant girl saw him seated there in the firelight. She looked closely at him and said, 'This man was with him.'

But he denied it. 'Woman, I don't know him,' he said.

A little later someone else saw him and said, 'You also are one of them.'

'Man, I am not!' Peter replied.

About an hour later another asserted, 'Certainly this fellow was with him, for he is a Galilean.'

Peter replied, 'Man, I don't know what you're talking about!' Just as he was speaking, the cock crowed. The Lord turned and looked straight at Peter. Then Peter remembered the word the Lord had spoken to him: 'Before the cock crows today, you will disown me three times.' And he went outside and wept bitterly. (Luke 22:54–62)

Think it through!

➤ Who had shown Peter that Jesus was 'the Christ, the Son of the living God'?

➤ Why did Jesus go on to speak to Peter as if he were Satan and describe him as 'a stumbling-block'?

- What did Peter struggle to comprehend?
- How does this help us to understand Peter's denial of Jesus?
- Did Jesus give up on Peter because he would betray Him?
- What does this tell us about the importance of understanding the meaning of Jesus' death?

14 An innocent man

By Pontius Pilate

Power: it is all I ever wanted. I spent years working for it and now I have it! Every morning, I walk around the flat roof of my palace and watch the city wake up and spring into life, reminding myself that I am the master of all I can see. However, recent events have made me wonder whether things are quite what they seem. In theory, I wield immense power—I rule an important part of the world—but an Emperor has put me in my position and I am answerable to him. He expects me to supervise his troops, collect taxes and keep order. If I do my job well, he rewards me, but if I fail, I might pay with my life. If rioting were to break out, my position would soon be threatened, and that is why law and order are my highest priorities.

It is now the busiest time of the year. Thousands of extra people are pouring into the city for a festival, reports of crime are widespread and murmurs about uprisings are being whispered under people's breath. I have taken the usual precautions: moving troops in from the countryside to bolster the number I have already stationed in the city, and paying informants to let me know of anything out of the ordinary. I have been told about a man who has been gathering huge crowds but, until now, he has given me no cause for concern. Apparently, he captivates people with stories, amazes them with his miracles, and teaches them about God. There is nothing to suggest he is a subversive; in fact, his message is about forgiveness and love. The people who worry me more are those who believe that God has promised to send them a King who will free them from our rule.

A few days ago, when Jesus arrived in the city, he was greeted as if he were the man who had come to do this. People flocked around him, declared their loyalty to him and laid down palms to make his ride more comfortable. But he didn't play the part of a war leader striding into a city to claim it as his own. A King would ride a horse, but he came on a donkey!

I have also had reports that the religious leaders are against him and that some of them are plotting to kill him. It is now late on Thursday night and things have taken a turn for the worse. My sources tell me that Jesus has disappeared and that the torches in the building where the council of religious leaders meets have been burning through the night. I have suddenly become aware of the limits of my power. These people have been given the right to govern religious matters and, if they decide to put Jesus on trial, there is nothing I can do. I cannot sleep, so I spend the night pacing the floor, waiting for news to come in.

At last, something is happening! One of my staff runs into my office to tell me that a group of religious leaders is heading towards my palace, and they have Jesus with them.

He is unlike any prisoner I have ever seen.

I look out and see the strange sight of these men, in their long, flowing gowns, leading him to my palace. He is unlike any prisoner I have ever seen. He is not trembling with fear or seething with hatred; in fact, you could almost think that he is in complete control of the situation. They read out their accusations against him: he is a subversive who opposes payment of taxes and claims to be the King their prophets have spoken about. 'Do you have anything to say?' I ask. He remains silent.

I look at the prisoner; he seems anything but a subversive, but everything like a King. 'Are you these people's King?' I ask. 'Yes, it is as you say,' he replies. I have heard enough! I turn to the religious leaders, noticing that a restless crowd has gathered around them. 'I find no basis for charging this man,' I say, with all the authority I can muster; but it is not enough. 'The things he has been teaching have stirred up people all over the region,' they say. 'That is what he was doing when he was in the north, and he's carrying it on down here.' I am so relieved to hear them talk about the north; it is outside my area of jurisdiction, so I can rid myself of this problem by sending Jesus to the Governor of the northern territories. I am going to bed now, relieved that I have defused a potentially dangerous situation, and satisfied with my political skill.

It is now early Friday morning, and I have been woken up by a frantic knock on the door. As I drift into consciousness, I can hear my servant's muffled voice: 'Governor, those religious men have returned and they have a message for you.' I quickly dress and come down to meet them. 'Why are you back?' I say angrily. 'I told you, this doesn't concern me because it started in the north!' My servant turns towards me and whispers, 'Sir, I think you'd better have a look at this before you say anything else.' He hands me a letter from Herod, who governs the north; it says, 'I cannot find anything wrong with this man, so I am sending him back to you.' I read it through and look up. 'Very well, you had better leave him with me.' They leave my palace, swelling the crowd that has gathered outside. After some quick thinking, I wonder whether I might have a solution: during this feast, it is my custom to release a prisoner. I can go over the heads of these religious men and tell the crowd that I will release Jesus.

I go out to address the crowd, confident that the people will welcome the offer of Jesus' release, but their mood is ugly. They demand I release a terrorist. 'Away with Jesus,' they snarl. I try a different approach and appeal for the crowd to let Jesus go free, but they are baying for his blood. 'Crucify him!' they chant over and over. I persist: 'Why? What crime has this man committed? I cannot find any reason to have him executed. I am going to have him punished and then I'll release him.' Surely this will satisfy them. The punishments handed out by my guards are ferocious: a prisoner is lashed with a whip with hooks on the end, and some men are even known to die from it. But it is not enough—the people want Jesus dead. They shout abuse and then say something that alarms me: 'If you release him, you are no friend of the Emperor's.' Whoever first voiced this must have known that my position is precarious. It strikes a chord with me; the Emperor wants order, and if I release Jesus, the crowd will riot. So I order the terrorist's release and Jesus' execution.

I have now returned to my office at the end of the blackest day of my life. My clever schemes have come to nothing, those religious men have outwitted me and my reputation is in tatters. Now quietness hangs over the city. The crowd has dispersed, Jesus has died and his body has been taken down from the cross. The danger of rioting has passed. I have survived the crisis, yet I feel dirty.

I have never met another man like him. He, a prisoner, made me feel as if I were on trial. I could see no trace of hate or fear in him, only compassion. If there was ever a truly innocent man, it was Jesus, and I was powerless to stop his execution.

THEN the Jews led Jesus from Caiaphas to the palace of the Roman governor. By now it was early morning, and to avoid ceremonial uncleanness the Jews did not enter the palace; they wanted to be able to eat the Passover. So Pilate came out to them and asked, 'What charges are you bringing against this man?'

'If he were not a criminal,' they replied, 'we would not have handed him over to you.'

Pilate said, 'Take him yourselves and judge him by your own law.'

'But we have no right to execute anyone,' the Jews objected. This happened so that the words Jesus had spoken indicating the kind of death he was going to die would be fulfilled.

Pilate then went back inside the palace, summoned Jesus and asked him, 'Are you the king of the Jews?'

'Is that your own idea,' Jesus asked, 'or did others talk to you about me?'

'Am I a Jew?' Pilate replied. 'It was your people and your chief priests who handed you over to me. What is it you have done?'

Jesus said, 'My kingdom is not of this world. If it were, my servants would fight to prevent my arrest by the Jews. But now my kingdom is from another place.'

'You are a king, then!' said Pilate.

Jesus answered, 'You are right in saying I am a king. In fact, for this reason I was born, and for this I came into the world, to testify to the truth. Everyone on the side of truth listens to me.'

'What is truth?' Pilate asked. With this he went out again to the Jews and said, 'I find no basis for a charge against him. But it is your custom for me to release to you one prisoner at the time of the Passover. Do you want me to release "the king of the Jews"?'

They shouted back, 'No, not him! Give us Barabbas!' Now Barabbas had taken part in a rebellion.

Then Pilate took Jesus and had him flogged. The soldiers twisted together a crown of thorns and put it on his head. They clothed him in a purple robe and went up to him again and again, saying, 'Hail, king of the Jews!' And they struck him in the face.

Once more Pilate came out and said to the Jews, 'Look, I am bringing him out to you to let you know that I find no basis for a charge against him.' When Jesus came out wearing the crown of thorns and the purple robe, Pilate said to them, 'Here is the man!'

As soon as the chief priests and their officials saw him, they shouted, 'Crucify! Crucify!'

But Pilate answered, 'You take him and crucify him. As for me, I find no basis for a charge against him.'

The Jews insisted, 'We have a law, and according to that law he must die, because he claimed to be the Son of God.'

When Pilate heard this, he was even more afraid, and he went back inside the palace. 'Where do you come from?' he asked Jesus, but Jesus gave him no answer. 'Do you refuse to speak to me?' Pilate said. 'Don't you realise I have power either to free you or to crucify you?'

Jesus answered, 'You would have no power over me if it were not given to you from above. Therefore the one who handed me over to you is guilty of a greater sin.'

From then on, Pilate tried to set Jesus free, but the Jews kept shouting, 'If you let this man go, you are no friend of Caesar. Anyone who claims to be a king opposes Caesar.'

When Pilate heard this, he brought Jesus out and sat down on the judge's seat at a place known as the Stone Pavement (which in Aramaic is Gabbatha). It was the day of Preparation of Passover Week, about the sixth hour.

'Here is your king,' Pilate said to the Jews.

But they shouted, 'Take him away! Take him away! Crucify him!'

'Shall I crucify your king?' Pilate asked.

'We have no king but Caesar,' the chief priests answered.

Finally Pilate handed him over to them to be crucified.

So the soldiers took charge of Jesus. (John 18:28–19:16)

Think it through!

➢ Why were the religious leaders taking Jesus to Pilate?

➢ How did this fulfil what Jesus had predicted was going to happen?

- The religious leaders wouldn't enter Pilate's house because some of the food in Pilate's kitchen was considered to be 'unclean' and contact with it would have stopped them from eating the Passover meal. How does this contrast with the reason for their visit?

- What does this tell us about the shallowness of their religion?

- Can you think of any parallels today?

- Look over Pilate's discussion with Jesus. What is the central theme?

- What makes Jesus' Kingship different from that of any other?

- What does Jesus tell Pilate about the Kingdom he came to establish?

- What is Pilate's declaration about the charges made against Jesus?

- Spend some time thinking about the significance of Pilate's question, 'Shall I crucify your King?' If Jesus is portrayed to us as a crucified King, how should His followers expect to be treated by the world?

- Who do the crowds choose as their King instead of Jesus? What is shocking about their statement?

15 Drama on death row

By **Jared Melchi***

Although it is all around me, death is a subject I have tried not to think about. Hardly a day goes by without news that someone I know has been wrenched from this world. A friend falls ill, or someone who seemed to have years of life stretching out before him suddenly dies. Sad as it is, I have decided to spend as little time thinking about death as possible. It awaits us all, so we might as well get on with life. However, this grim Friday morning, I find myself staring death in the face.

Having slept fitfully, I wake up as soon as a chink of morning light breaks into my cell. For one delightful moment, I can't quite think where I am, but the reality of my circumstances soon storms its way into my mind. I am in a condemned man's cell, awaiting execution. This is going to be the last day of my life.

There has been a lot of coming and going during the night and it seems to be related to something I can hear going on in the distance. At first, I thought it was the crowd, which had descended on the city for the festival, but it was different from their busy hum; it was restless and unhappy. The guards outside my cell seem excited about something that is going on at the Governor's Palace. Whenever people come in, they ask if there is any more news. I can't quite hear everything that is being said, but it sounds as if a popular figure has fallen out of favour, been tried by the religious leaders, and then brought to the Governor for execution.

The first few hours of the morning pass with eerie slowness. I spend the time reflecting on my short life, reliving happy memories and repressing the dread of the ordeal that lies ahead of me, but my time finally arrives. The prison door opens, two guards grab me roughly and lead me out. I emerge from the darkness screwing up my eyes from the sudden burst of morning sun. When they adjust, I see another prisoner being led in the same direction. I look towards him, but as I do so, a guard hits me around the head and tells me to look directly in front.

> **Jesus seemed unstoppable. Everyone was talking about his miracles.**

The nearer I get to the site of my execution, the more I become aware of an ugly sound, similar to what I heard during the night: a crowd demanding a man's death. But who are they calling out for? It can't be me; I am just a common thief. Perhaps the other person taking this terrifying journey is a notorious criminal who is hated and feared.

My ears are pounding and my heart is racing as the place of my execution comes into sight. I see a third person being led to his death and realize that the crowd has been screaming at him and not me. I wonder who he is. Perhaps he is a murderer, or a leader who has abused his position and committed terrible crimes. Then I see his face—covered in blood and bruises, but still recognizable. It is Jesus, the great teacher who performs miracles.

Having been locked away, I have no idea of the circumstances that have brought about this shocking turn of events. Just a matter of days ago, when I was a free man, Jesus seemed unstoppable. Everyone was talking about his miracles and the way in which he was greeted with such rapture as he rode into the city on a donkey. What could he have possibly done to deserve execution?

The three of us are nailed onto pieces of wood made in a cross shape, and the crosses are dropped into the ground, agony searing through our bodies as they jolt into position. I scream in pain, the other man curses, but Jesus—already smarting from a brutal beating—is silent. We are put either side of him. I listen to the roar of the crowd and I try to pick out words and phrases that might give me some kind of idea as to the reason for Jesus' execution. I hear people bellow out things like, 'He saved others, let him save himself— that's if he's the King God has sent us, the chosen one', their voices resonating with hatred, their faces disfigured by ugly sneers. I'm not sure whether they are able to hear Jesus' response above the noise they are making, but I can, and I find it so moving that, for an instant, I forget about my own pain. He is praying for them. 'Father, forgive them,' he says, 'they do not know what they are doing.' But they seem so intoxicated with their unleashed venom that they are oblivious to these amazing words.

Jesus: the life changer

The soldiers decide to join in with them, sarcastically offering Jesus a drink to take the pain away. 'If you are the King of the Jews, save yourself,' they say. The other man being executed looks towards Jesus. Gasping for breath, seething with bitterness and racked with pain, he asks, 'Are you the King? Save yourself and us!' It is obvious that Jesus has done nothing wrong, and even in the injustice of his death he displays love and compassion. I muster up every last ounce of energy I have left and call out to the other man, 'Don't you fear God? We are getting what we deserve. But this man has done nothing wrong!' Then I look at the tortured, yet composed, face of the man stretched out on the cross next to me.

If this man is the King we have been waiting for, even the cross will not stop him.

Surely, if there was ever a King who has been promised to us, it is him! 'Jesus,' I say, 'remember me when you come into your Kingdom.' If this man is the King we have been waiting for, even the cross will not stop him—somehow, some day, he will come back in power. That seems a long way in the distance, but I want to be part of it and I believe it will happen. And he takes me by surprise again. I spoke in terms of the distant future—but he talks about the present: 'I tell you,' he says, 'today you will be with me in paradise.' I can hardly take in what I have just heard! Death no longer seems the end—it is just the beginning of something much better! I look up and whisper a few words of prayer, thanking God that my last hours have been spent with Jesus, the King he promised to send to us.

TWO other men, both criminals, were also led out with him to be executed. When they came to the place called the Skull, there they crucified him, along with the criminals—one on his right, the other on his left. Jesus said, 'Father, forgive them, for they do not know what they are doing.' And they divided up his clothes by casting lots.

The people stood watching, and the rulers even sneered at him. They said, 'He saved others; let him save himself if he is the Christ of God, the Chosen One.'

The soldiers also came up and mocked him. They offered him wine vinegar and said, 'If you are the king of the Jews, save yourself.'

There was a written notice above him, which read: THIS IS THE KING OF THE JEWS.

One of the criminals who hung there hurled insults at him: 'Aren't you the Christ? Save yourself and us!'

But the other criminal rebuked him. 'Don't you fear God,' he said, 'since you are under the same sentence? We are punished justly, for we are getting what our deeds deserve. But this man has done nothing wrong.'

Then he said, 'Jesus, remember me when you come into your kingdom.'

Jesus answered him, 'I tell you the truth, today you will be with me in paradise.' (Luke 23:32–43)

Think it through!

- Think of some words that would describe Jesus' attitude while He was dying on the cross.

- Look at the insults the crowds and the soldiers shouted at Jesus. What idea were they attacking?

MORE STUDY QUESTIONS ▶

Jesus: the life changer

- What hadn't they understood?
- How different from this was the attitude of the criminal who said, 'this man has done nothing wrong'?
- What was Jesus' response to him?
- What does this teach us about faith in Jesus?
- How does this man's attitude compare with your own?

16 The case of the torn curtain

By **Levi Barzillai***

When my friends and I get together, we usually talk about our jobs. Samuel, a farmer, tells us how his crops are growing; Jacob, a tradesman, speaks endlessly about the different people he meets in the market place; Andrew, a craftsman, describes his latest project; and I tell everyone about the man I work for. My friends are always interested in this subject because he is the Chief Priest.

When I tell people that I am his personal assistant, responsible for making sure that he has everything he needs, their eyes widen, they sit up straight and they ask me what it's like to work for 'such a holy man'. I used to tell them how impressive he was. He was disciplined, devoted to God, and caring. He had a sense of purpose and spoke about the privilege of enabling people to present sacrifices to God so that they could be forgiven of their sins. But in the last few years, I have seen a gradual but noticeable change. It began when the name 'Jesus' kept coming up in conversations. People described him as a skilful teacher, a compelling speaker, a miracle-worker, even a Prophet. Initially, the Chief Priest was interested to hear about Jesus, but his curiosity turned to concern when people began to compare Jesus with the religious leaders and say things like: 'He teaches us with such authority; why can't the teachers in the Temple be the same?'

> **The Chief Priest was interested to hear about Jesus, but his curiosity turned to concern when people began to compare Jesus with the religious leaders.**

Then came the visit of the Pharisees, the most zealous of all our religious leaders. They saw themselves as the guardians of the law; they believed it

98 Jesus: the life changer

was their responsibility to maintain the standards that God had laid down. They had even added extra rules and regulations to the laws that already existed. When they arrived at the Temple door, asking to see the Chief Priest, they looked angry and agitated. I carried on with my duties while they spoke to him, and I caught some of the things they were saying. 'Jesus broke the commandments when he healed someone on the Sabbath.'[14] They said he was dangerous and that he must be stopped; and when I glanced in their direction, I could see the Chief Priest nodding in agreement.

That day was the turning point. From then on, the Chief Priest became less caring and more confrontational; he was often distracted and agitated. Every so often he would have a visit from a group of Pharisees and they would huddle into a corner and talk in whispers. I tried to get as near to them as I could, so that I could hear what they were saying. I could only manage to catch a few sentences—'we can't risk a riot', 'he's too popular for that', 'not at Passover time, it's too dangerous'.

Passover is the busiest time of the year in the Temple. People flock into the city, the Chief Priest makes sure everything is in place, and I have to follow him wherever he goes so that I can help him in any way he needs. This year, things were different. There was another visit from the Pharisees and they had a long discussion with the Chief Priest. The name 'Judas' was mentioned; they spoke about a golden opportunity that they couldn't let pass, and then left, with hatred written all over their faces. After that, the Chief Priest seemed to be preoccupied and abrupt. Something was going on, but I couldn't work out what it might be.

They spoke about a golden opportunity that they couldn't let pass, and then left, with hatred written all over their faces.

I usually look forward to Passover. The city is buzzing with excitement and pilgrims arrive, full of enthusiasm and expectation. It is a time to remember God's deliverance, celebrate his goodness, and ask for his forgiveness. Somehow it seemed different this year. A massive crowd had gathered in a part of the city, demanding Jesus' execution. The atmosphere was tense, people were agitated, and the Roman soldiers seemed to be extra vigilant in stamping out any sign of trouble. Then, in the middle of the day, the most extraordinary thing happened—everything went dark. It was just like when you blow out a candle at the end of a day. And it was dark for so long that I wondered whether it would ever get light again. But hours later, the light returned. There was a sense of relief, an attempt to get back to normality, and a few suggestions as to what could have been behind the darkness. And then someone pointed towards the most sacred place in the Temple and gasped: the huge, thick curtain that separated people like me from the area where the Priest offered sacrifices was ripped from top to bottom. We could look right into it and see things considered to be too sacred for our eyes. The Chief Priest told us to look away and a makeshift replacement was put up, but no one could explain how it had happened. There were no signs of any knife or sword having been used—it was torn. But how could anyone have done it? The material was too thick and heavy for the strongest man to even attempt such a thing.

Later on, I found out that the darkness fell and the curtain was ripped just as Jesus died. I had heard that, when he began to preach, John, the man who preached in the desert, described him as 'the Lamb of God, who takes away the sin of the world'.[15] During the years I have worked in the Temple, I have seen thousands of lambs brought for sacrifice. People lay their hands on them, which symbolizes their sins being transferred to the animals so that they can be offered to God. The lambs look so innocent, and the people wear such guilty expressions as they hand them over. It seems sad to have blameless creatures killed, but I tell myself that this is the cost of forgiveness. After that dark Friday, I heard stories of Jesus' love and his words of dignity as he went to his death. The image of those lambs came straight into my mind. Jesus had said, 'I am the way and the truth and the life. No one comes to the Father except through me.'[16] Every day, I could see the way to God blocked by that curtain. And while I could seek forgiveness and pray, only a Priest could enter into God's presence and secure forgiveness for me. Perhaps that rip in the curtain was an act of God, a statement that things will change because Jesus has made it possible for us to approach God.

It seemed as if the world had ended when the darkness wrapped itself around us, but when the sun broke through, it was like a new beginning. Things would be different, God would be nearer, darkness would be broken, and worship would be more joyful.

Now there are claims that Jesus has risen from the dead, and his followers are telling us about a new relationship with God brought about by Jesus. I am going to find out more!

AT the sixth hour darkness came over the whole land until the ninth hour. And at the ninth hour Jesus cried out in a loud voice, 'Eloi, Eloi, lama sabachthani?'—which means, 'My God, my God, why have you forsaken me?'

When some of those standing near heard this, they said, 'Listen, he's calling Elijah.'

One man ran, filled a sponge with wine vinegar, put it on a stick, and offered it to Jesus to drink. 'Now leave him alone. Let's see if Elijah comes to take him down,' he said.

With a loud cry, Jesus breathed his last.

The curtain of the temple was torn in two from top to bottom. And when the centurion, who stood there in front of Jesus, heard his cry and saw how he died, he said, 'Surely this man was the Son of God!'

Some women were watching from a distance. Among them were Mary Magdalene, Mary the mother of James the younger and of Joses [Barnabas], and Salome. In Galilee these women had followed him and cared for his needs. Many other women who had come up with him to Jerusalem were also there. (Mark 15:33–41)

Think it through!

➢ Think about the significance of the darkness that fell as Jesus died.

➢ The curtain separated everyone but the Priest from the Most Holy part of the temple (and he was only able to

MORE STUDY QUESTIONS ➤

Jesus: the life changer

go there once a year). What statement was God making when it was torn?

- What was happening when Jesus died on the cross? The following verses from the New Testament will help you to think about this:

    > God made him who had no sin to be sin for us, so that in him we might become the righteousness of God. (2 Corinthians 5:21)

    > He himself bore our sins in his body on the tree, so that we might die to sins and live for righteousness; by his wounds you have been healed. (1 Peter 2:24)

- Why did Jesus cry out, 'My God, my God, why have you forsaken me'?

- What do each of the verses below tell us about the response we need to make to Jesus' death and resurrection?

    > Then he opened their minds so they could understand the Scriptures. He told them, 'This is what is written: The Christ will suffer and rise from the dead on the third day, and repentance and forgiveness of sins will be preached in his name to all nations, beginning at Jerusalem.' (Luke 24:45–47)

    > If you confess with your mouth, 'Jesus is Lord,' and believe in your heart that God raised him from the dead, you will be saved. (Romans 10:9)

    > For it is by grace you have been saved, through faith—and this not from yourselves, it is the gift of God—not by works, so that no one can boast. (Ephesians 2:8)

    > Yet to all who received him, to those who believed in his name, he gave the right to become children of God—children born not of natural descent, nor of human decision or a husband's will, but born of God. (John 1:12–13)

17 From desperation to celebration

By **Amos Joses***

Have you ever been shut in a room with people who are locked in deep discussion, and had the urge to get out and go for a walk? There is something about getting beyond the suffocating presence of four walls and using up some energy that may help you think a little more clearly. And after the ordeal we had been through, this was something I desperately needed!

It was Sunday, the first day of the week, and the people of Jerusalem seemed to have forgotten about the bloodletting of Friday and were getting on with their lives. The clatter of footsteps, the hum of conversation and the noise of traders going about their business outside the room we hid in seemed to heighten our sense of isolation and make the events of the past few days seem unreal. When I listened hard, I could pick out the things people were talking about—everyday matters such as their families and their work. Surely some of these ordinary people had been part of that ugly mob assembled on the hill where Jesus was crucified. How could they get on with their lives as if nothing had happened? Occasionally, you would hear someone express an opinion: 'Jesus meant well, but he couldn't bring us freedom. Anyway, how could he have been the King God promised us if he let himself get crucified?'

> **When he rode into Jerusalem to such an enthusiastic welcome, I felt so privileged to be one of his followers.**

I had some sympathy with what they were saying. I had believed with all my heart that Jesus was the King we were waiting for. When he rode into Jerusalem to such an enthusiastic welcome, I felt so privileged to be one of his followers; I thought that the next few days were going to be the most exciting I had ever known and that Jesus was going to establish his Kingdom. But a week later, excitement had given way to despair. Instead of a coronation, there was a crucifixion. Jesus was dead, and my hopes and dreams had died with him. I had so many questions. If he was a King, why was he killed so brutally? What made those people turn against him so suddenly and viciously? Why did one of his followers betray him? What were we to make of the things he had been teaching us? What should we do now that he was dead?

Of course, I was not the only person asking these questions. All eleven of us, who had been with Jesus for three eventful years, were struggling with them. But, although we talked at great length, reliving the brutal events of the past few days, we had no answers to those painful questions. The room was full of heavy sighs and bitter tears; it felt almost as if the walls were closing in on us.

Suddenly, the door burst open; our eyes darted towards it, for fear of who it might be. It was two of the women, Mary and Martha, who had been to tend to the body of Jesus. I didn't think it could get any worse, but my heart sank even further. Surely they were not going to tell us that Jesus' tomb had been desecrated. But their faces were not drawn like ours: they were actually smiling, and they had something they couldn't wait to tell us. Mary and Martha seemed more like excited children than women who had lost someone they dearly loved. 'The tomb is empty!' they said. 'We saw an angel and he told us that Jesus has risen from the dead!' A stunned silence came over the room; part of me wanted to believe them, but I wasn't going to let myself suffer another disappointment. 'Let's calm down and think about this carefully,' said John. 'Are you sure about this?' 'Yes!' they said in unison. John looked over to Peter: 'We'd better go and take a look, then,' he said, displaying little hope that their story might be true.

> **Part of me wanted to believe them, but I wasn't going to let myself suffer another disappointment.**

John and Peter seemed to be gone for hours. We paced the floor to use up our nervous energy; we suppressed our desperate hopes and kept looking out the window to see if they were coming back.

When they finally arrived, they were walking, not running, and frowning, not smiling. Their footsteps were heavy as they came up the stairs, and we prepared ourselves for the worst; those women must have let their imaginations run away with them. The door creaked open and the two men entered slowly. 'What's the news, then?' I asked. 'Well,' said Peter, 'the tomb is empty, but we saw neither Jesus nor the angel the women told us about.'

We slumped in our seats and buried our heads in our hands. After a few moments, I looked up and tapped Cleopas on the shoulder. I suggested that it might be better if we got out of the room and headed away from Jerusalem. It was early afternoon, the midday heat had passed, and there was no point hanging around in this oppressive atmosphere any longer.

We walked through the winding streets and left Jerusalem. After walking for another twenty-five minutes, we reached the edge of the plateau and looked back towards the place where our hopes had been shattered. A little later, we were on the road that leads to a town called Emmaus. Although we felt free of the tense atmosphere that had filled that little room, we carried on talking about the events of the past week. We spoke about the way in which the religious leaders had orchestrated Jesus' trial and execution. The crowd had turned so ugly, we'd let Jesus down so badly, and he had gone through the whole ordeal with such dignity. Those who were brave enough to stay at the site of the execution told us that he actually prayed for the people who were cursing him, asking God to forgive them.

We didn't know who he was, but he seemed to be very interested in our conversation.

Cleopas and I were so absorbed in conversation that we hadn't noticed someone walking beside us. We didn't know who he was, but he seemed to be very interested in our conversation. 'What are you talking about?' he asked. We stood still and looked at him with amazement, our faces ravaged by the misery of the previous four days. How could he have come from Jerusalem and not known what was going on? 'You must be the only person who doesn't know what's been happening over the last few days,' said Cleopas. 'What do you mean?' he replied. We seized on this opportunity to tell someone outside our circle about the things we had been struggling with. We began by telling him about Jesus, describing him as a mighty prophet who was favoured by God and recognized by the people. Then we told him about the way in which the religious leaders had arrested him, condemned him to death and handed him over to the Governor for

106 Jesus: the life changer

execution. And we brought our account right up to date by telling him about the glimmer of hope brought by the women, who told us that his tomb was empty: a hope that was dashed when Peter and John returned and told us that, although Jesus' body had indeed gone, there was no sign of the angels the women claimed to have spoken to.

After pouring out our hearts to this stranger, we expected some sympathy, but we didn't get it!

After pouring out our hearts to this stranger, we expected some sympathy, but we didn't get it! 'You are such foolish people!' he said. 'You find it so hard to believe what the Prophets wrote. Didn't they predict that the King God promised would have to suffer all these things before he began his rule?' He went on to talk about the Scriptures—his knowledge of them was amazing! He went right back to the law, telling us how the sacrifices and offerings anticipated the King's suffering. Then he told us about the way in which the Prophets and Psalms spoke of the same thing. We were right to expect the King to be glorious, but first he had to suffer.

For the first time in days we were lifted out of the blackness which had engulfed us. This man's words made sense and he gave us hope; and we were so taken up with what he was saying that we were hardly aware of time passing. We had trodden all seven miles of that long road, but with the new sense of hope he had given us, we would gladly have gone twice the distance to hear more.

When we arrived at Emmaus, the stranger acted as if he was going further. It was late, so we urged him to stay with us, and he accepted the offer. Food was set out and we asked him to thank God for it. He agreed, picked up a small loaf of bread, asked God to bless it, broke it into pieces, and then handed them out to us. It is difficult to explain what happened next. It was like those times when you have not been able to see very well because of something wrong with your eyes, and then they suddenly improve. Everything seems hazy and clouded, and then suddenly you can see clearly. In an instant, we both realized that we were sharing a meal with Jesus. It was as if God had hidden his identity from us and then opened our eyes. I looked at Cleopas, he looked at me, and we both looked back to Jesus—but he had gone. But it didn't matter to us; we knew that he had risen from the dead and he had taught us that his death was not an accident: it had been planned long ago and set out in the Scriptures. It was God's plan for his Son to die on the cross and rise from the dead. 'Didn't it seem as if your heart was burning with hope when he explained the Scriptures to us?' we asked each other.

Although the day was drawing to a close, we could not stay in Emmaus: we were bursting with joy and had to get back to tell the others. So, within the hour, we were on our way back to Jerusalem. Our new sense of purpose and joy infused us with energy and we got there in half the time of our first journey. After running through the streets of the city, we raced up the stairs and burst into the room. We expected the others to be in the black mood they were in when we left them, but we could not have been more wrong. They were bristling with a joyful energy too, and before we could give them our news, they told us theirs: 'It's true, the Lord has risen! Peter has met with him!'

ON the first day of the week, very early in the morning, the women took the spices they had prepared and went to the tomb. They found the stone rolled away from the tomb, but when they entered, they did not find the body of the Lord Jesus. While they were wondering about this, suddenly two men in clothes that gleamed like lightning stood beside them. In their fright the women bowed down with their faces to the ground, but the men said to them, 'Why do you look for the living among the dead? He is not here; he has risen! Remember how he told you, while he was still with you in Galilee: "The Son of Man must be delivered into the hands of sinful men, be crucified and on the third day be raised again."' Then they remembered his words.

When they came back from the tomb, they told all these things to the Eleven and to all the others. It was Mary Magdalene, Joanna, Mary the mother of James, and the others with them who told this to the apostles. But they did not believe the women, because their words seemed to them like nonsense. Peter, however, got up and ran to the tomb. Bending over, he saw the strips of linen lying by themselves, and he went away, wondering to himself what had happened.

Now that same day two of them were going to a village called Emmaus, about seven miles from Jerusalem. They were talking with each other about everything that had happened. As they talked and discussed these things with each other, Jesus himself came up and walked along with them; but they were kept from recognising him.

He asked them, 'What are you discussing together as you walk along?'

They stood still, their faces downcast. One of them, named Cleopas, asked him, 'Are you only a visitor to Jerusalem and do not know the things that have happened there in these days?'

'What things?' he asked.

'About Jesus of Nazareth,' they replied. 'He was a prophet, powerful in word and deed before God and all the people. The chief priests and our rulers handed him over to be sentenced to death, and they crucified him; but we had hoped that he was the one who was going to redeem Israel. And what is more, it is the third day since all this took place. In addition, some of our women amazed us. They went to the tomb early this morning but didn't find his body.

They came and told us that they had seen a vision of angels, who said he was alive. Then some of our companions went to the tomb and found it just as the women had said, but him they did not see.'

He said to them, 'How foolish you are, and how slow of heart to believe all that the prophets have spoken! Did not the Christ have to suffer these things and then enter his glory?' And beginning with Moses and all the Prophets, he explained to them what was said in all the Scriptures concerning himself.

As they approached the village to which they were going, Jesus acted as if he were going further. But they urged him strongly, 'Stay with us, for it is nearly evening; the day is almost over.' So he went in to stay with them.

When he was at the table with them, he took bread, gave thanks, broke it and began to give it to them. Then their eyes were opened and they recognised him, and he disappeared from their sight. They asked each other, 'Were not our hearts burning within us while he talked with us on the road and opened the Scriptures to us?'

They got up and returned at once to Jerusalem. There they found the Eleven and those with them, assembled together and saying, 'It is true! The Lord has risen and has appeared to Simon.' Then the two told what had happened on the way, and how Jesus was recognised by them when he broke the bread.

While they were still talking about this, Jesus himself stood among them and said to them, 'Peace be with you.'

They were startled and frightened, thinking they saw a ghost. He said to them, 'Why are you troubled, and why do doubts rise in your minds? Look at my hands and my feet. It is I myself! Touch me and see; a ghost does not have flesh and bones, as you see I have.'

When he had said this, he showed them his hands and feet. And while they still did not believe it because of joy and amazement, he asked them, 'Do you have anything here to eat?' They gave him a piece of broiled fish, and he took it and ate it in their presence.

He said to them, 'This is what I told you while I was still with you: Everything must be fulfilled that is written about me in the Law of Moses, the Prophets and the Psalms.'

Then he opened their minds so they could understand the Scriptures. He told them, 'This is what is written: The Christ will suffer and rise from the dead on the third day, and repentance and forgiveness of sins will be preached in his name to all nations, beginning at Jerusalem. You are witnesses of these things. I am going to send you what my Father has promised; but stay in the city until you have been clothed with power from on high.' (Luke 24:1–49)

Think it through!

- What do the angels draw Mary and Martha's attention to?
- Why do you think the disciples travelling to Emmaus were 'kept from recognising' Jesus?

MORE STUDY QUESTIONS ▶

- Describe the hopes they had invested in Jesus.
- How had these hopes been dashed?
- Where had the disciples gone wrong in their thinking?
- What does Jesus draw their attention to?
- What does this tell us about Jesus' place in the Bible?
- Can we understand the message of the Bible without grasping the meaning of Jesus' death and resurrection?
- How does Jesus enable the disciples to understand the Scriptures? Can we expect the same kind of help?

18 A change of tone

By **Thomas Didymus**

There are many things I have regretted saying, but nothing more so than the comments I made shortly after Jesus' death. We had been Jesus' constant companions for the past three years, following him as he taught people about God's Kingdom and healed their illnesses. He had been taken from us, framed for a crime he did not commit and executed in the most hideous way you could imagine, creating a gaping void in our lives. Originally, there were twelve of us, but one, having betrayed Jesus, then committed suicide. The rest of us felt as if our hearts had been ripped open. There was the shock of losing Jesus in such a brutal way, the pain of separation, the loss of our leader and our regret that we had not stood with him in his hour of need. We shut ourselves in a room, wallowing in regret. 'I can still hear him saying, "Couldn't you wait up with me for one hour?"' someone said, shaking his head in disbelief at the events which had overtaken us. 'I let him down, and I cannot forgive myself.'

> **There are many things I have regretted saying, but nothing more so than the comments I made shortly after Jesus' death.**

The atmosphere had become so suffocating that I decided to go out and take a walk. As I padded along the streets, I could hardly believe that many of the people milling about were part of the mob venting its hatred at Jesus three days ago. Now they'd had their entertainment, they were getting on with their lives, while we were left devastated and bewildered. I glanced at their faces: they were ordinary, honest people. Did they realize what they had been part of? Were they aware of the way the religious leaders had manipulated them?

For most of the time, I wandered

around aimlessly, and eventually I went back to the room where my friends were. I walked up the stairs as slowly as possible, mentally preparing myself for the misery I expected to find. But the further I got up the steps, the more I became aware of the sound of excited chatter. 'They have changed their tone a bit,' I thought. 'How can they sound so cheerful when Jesus has gone?' As soon as the others saw me, they greeted me as if I was a late arrival at a family wedding. 'Guess what?' one of them said, with a huge smile on his face. 'We have seen the Master!' What were they talking about? Did they actually believe that Jesus had been with them? Had they forgotten he had been killed?

I looked at them, my mouth wide open and my eyes glazed. 'Can you tell me that again?' I said, as calmly as I possibly could. They repeated their astounding claim with added detail. They had not seen a ghost: Jesus was real, he was with them, he had risen from the dead. His resurrected body was extraordinary, enabling him to come through the doors which had been locked for fear of the Jews. He had stood among them, saying, 'Peace be with you'; he had showed them his hands and side; and he had breathed on them, giving them new power. My friends seemed to be energized with joy and dazed by the experience they described, so I tried to bring them down to earth. 'I won't believe it unless I see the nail wounds in his hands, put my fingers into them, and place my hand into the wound in his side.'[17]

How could they expect me to be so happy about something I had not seen for myself?

I realize how disparaging that might sound, but try to understand my position. I had been out of the room. At the time I left, they were drowning in despair, but when I came back, they were bubbling over with joy. How could they expect me to be so happy about something I had not seen for myself? But the events which unfolded showed how foolish I was. I would not take the word of eleven witnesses; I refused to believe them unless I could see Jesus for myself. And after eight long days, I did. The doors were still locked, but Jesus came through them; he stood among us and said, 'Peace be with you.' Then he turned and spoke to me: 'Put your finger here; see my hands. Reach out your hand and put it into my side. Stop doubting and believe.'[18]

If the sight of Jesus were not enough, his words filled me with wonder. He was aware of the discussion that had been going on in that little room eight

Jesus: the life changer

days earlier, even though he had not been physically present. And he knew what had been in my heart and mind. My response was short but heartfelt: 'My Master, my God!'

Our encounters with Jesus were unique and I would not want to lead you to expect quite the same thing. But when Jesus appeared to me, he told me something about people like you: 'You have believed me because you have seen me,' he said. 'Happy are those who have not seen and yet have believed.'

NOW Thomas (called Didymus), one of the Twelve, was not with the disciples when Jesus came. So the other disciples told him, 'We have seen the Lord!'

But he said to them, 'Unless I see the nail marks in his hands and put my finger where the nails were, and put my hand into his side, I will not believe it.'

A week later his disciples were in the house again, and Thomas was with them. Though the doors were locked, Jesus came and stood among them and said, 'Peace be with you!' Then he said to Thomas, 'Put your finger here; see my hands. Reach out your hand and put it into my side. Stop doubting and believe.'

Thomas said to him, 'My Lord and my God!'

Then Jesus told him, 'Because you have seen me, you have believed; blessed are those who have not seen and yet have believed.' (John 20:24–29)

Think it through!

➤ Why was it important for Thomas to be a witness of Jesus' resurrection? The verses below, in which the apostles set out the criteria for Judas' replacement, will help you to think about this:

MORE STUDY QUESTIONS ➤

Jesus: the life changer

'Therefore it is necessary to choose one of the men who have been with us the whole time the Lord Jesus went in and out among us, beginning from John's baptism to the time when Jesus was taken up from us. For one of these must become a witness with us of his resurrection.' (Acts 1:21–22)

- Of precisely what did Thomas want to see proof?
- How did Jesus respond to Thomas' wish when He appeared to him?
- Where do we find evidence of Jesus' resurrection?
- Why is the resurrection of Jesus such an important part of the good news about Jesus?
- How do Jesus' words to Thomas encourage us?

19 A look back in wonder

By **Nathaniel Justus***

The sun had risen and set fifty times since that eventful festival. The travellers had left, the population of the city had shrunk back to its usual size and life was going on as normal. There was still talk about Jesus because his followers were saying that he had come back from the dead; there was even a claim that five hundred people saw him at one time.[19] However, I was sceptical. The image of a man I had seen on the eve of Jesus' execution was still embedded in my mind. A group of people had been huddled round a fire, united in their desire to keep warm. One of them was recognized as a friend of Jesus, but when he was challenged about this, he said that he had never even known him. A little later, I saw this man again. He was talking to someone else who had recognized him. 'You're one of Jesus' group,' he said, but the man fiercely denied it.

Fifty days later, our city was in the thick of another festival. It was like a breath of fresh air, eliminating the foul odour of mob rule which had led to Jesus' execution. The city was full of people and humming with the sound of different languages. I wandered through the streets lapping up the atmosphere, amusing myself by trying to work out the places that people had come from and the distances they had travelled. The further I walked, the denser the crowd became, until I came to a complete standstill, discovering that a huge throng had gathered to listen to someone speak.

The sight of a mass of people brought back memories of the vicious mob that had gathered at the last festival, but this time the mood was different. They were listening intently to a man who was addressing them. I had not seen such a thing since Jesus first came into the city! I pressed my way through to get a good look at him. I couldn't believe what I saw—the speaker was the man I had seen the day before Jesus was executed!

It was hard to believe that this was the same person. He spoke with a passion and authority that reminded me of Jesus himself.

He started by telling us that God had endorsed Jesus by doing miracles through him. Until recently, I had associated Jesus with his miracles and teaching, but during the past fifty days I had begun to think of him as someone who had suffered a terrible, unjust death. The man talking to the crowd did not see it that way; he said that Jesus' death was part of God's pre-arranged plan.

He spoke with a passion and authority that reminded me of Jesus himself.

I had found the reports of Jesus' execution very moving. People spoke of the dignity with which he endured the barracking of the crowds, the beatings from the soldiers and the agony of crucifixion. I could not understand this; how could anyone show this kind of composure in circumstances so barbaric and unfair? But now it began to make sense: Jesus knew there was a purpose to his death.

What about the reports that Jesus had come back from the dead? As far as the speaker was concerned, they were more than mere claims—they were facts! He told us that God had released Jesus 'from the agony of death' and had brought him back to life again. Death could not keep its hold over him. Then he quoted a song written by David, one of our great Kings:

'I saw the Lord always before me. Because he is at my right hand, I will not be shaken. Therefore my heart is glad and my tongue rejoices; my body also will live in hope, because you will not abandon me to the grave, nor will you let your Holy One see decay.'[20]

'David is not talking about himself!' the man shouted triumphantly. 'He is dead and buried. Some of you have even visited his tomb! He had a glimpse of the future and saw one of his descendants who would rule in his place—a King who was not going to be left among the dead, or decompose in the grave. The man he is talking about is Jesus, whom God has raised from the dead. And now he has the highest place of honour in heaven!'

What a turn of events! The battered yet serene figure who hung on a cross, racked with pain but filled with purpose, had come back from the dead. He had appeared to hundreds of people, been taken up to heaven, and now sits at God's right hand.

Along with thousands of others, I felt as if a knife had been thrust into my heart. 'What shall we do?' asked an anguished member of the crowd. The speaker left us in no doubt as to what our response should be: 'Every one of you must turn from his sins and turn to God.'

From that moment, Jesus became the person I completely relied on for the forgiveness of sins. My life was changed—that's why I can now look back in wonder!

THEN Peter stood up with the Eleven, raised his voice and addressed the crowd: 'Fellow Jews and all of you who live in Jerusalem, let me explain this to you; listen carefully to what I say. These men are not drunk, as you suppose. It's only nine in the morning! No, this is what was spoken by the prophet Joel: "In the last days, God says, I will pour out my Spirit on all people. Your sons and daughters will prophesy, your young men will see visions, your old men will dream dreams. Even on my servants, both men and women, I will pour out my Spirit in those days, and they will prophesy. I will show wonders in the heaven above and signs on the earth below, blood and fire and billows of smoke. The sun will be turned to darkness and the moon to blood before the coming of the great and glorious day of the Lord. And everyone who calls on the name of the Lord will be saved."

'Men of Israel, listen to this: Jesus of Nazareth was a man accredited by God to you by miracles, wonders and signs, which God did among you through him, as you yourselves know. This man was handed over to you by God's set purpose and foreknowledge; and you, with the help of wicked men, put him to death by nailing him to the cross. But God raised him from the dead, freeing him from the agony of death, because it was impossible for death to keep its hold on him. David said about him: "I saw the Lord always before me. Because he is at my right hand, I will not be shaken. Therefore my heart is glad and my tongue rejoices; my body also will live in hope, because you will not abandon me to the grave, nor will you let your Holy One see decay. You have made known to me the paths of life; you will fill me with joy in your presence."

'Brothers, I can tell you confidently that the patriarch David died and was buried, and his tomb is here to this day. But he was a prophet and knew that God had promised him on oath that he would place one of his descendants on his throne. Seeing what was ahead, he spoke of the resurrection of the Christ, that he was not abandoned to the grave, nor did his body see decay. God has raised this Jesus to life, and we are all witnesses of the fact. Exalted to the right hand of God, he has received from the Father the promised Holy Spirit and has poured out what you now see and hear. For David did not ascend to heaven, and yet he said, "The Lord said to my Lord: 'Sit at my right hand until I make your enemies a footstool for your feet.'"

'Therefore let all Israel be assured of this: God has made this Jesus, whom you crucified, both Lord and Christ.'

When the people heard this, they were cut to the heart and said to Peter and the other apostles, 'Brothers, what shall we do?'

Peter replied, 'Repent and be baptised, every one of you, in the name of Jesus Christ for the forgiveness of your sins. And you will receive the gift of the Holy Spirit. The promise is for you and your children and for all who are far off—for all whom the Lord our God will call.'

With many other words he warned them; and he pleaded with them, 'Save yourselves from this corrupt generation.' Those who accepted his message were baptised, and about three thousand were added to their number that day. (Acts 2:14–41)

Think it through!

> What does Peter say concerning God's will and Jesus' crucifixion?

> Does this excuse the people who plotted against Him and those who put Him on the cross?

- Peter quotes from a psalm in the Old Testament and says that David, the writer, saw what was ahead and spoke of Christ's resurrection. He explains this more fully in his first letter:

  > Concerning this salvation, the prophets, who spoke of the grace that was to come to you, searched intently and with the greatest care, trying to find out the time and circumstances to which the Spirit of Christ in them was pointing when he predicted the sufferings of Christ and the glories that would follow. It was revealed to them that they were not serving themselves but you, when they spoke of the things that have now been told you by those who have preached the gospel to you by the Holy Spirit sent from heaven. Even angels long to look into these things. (1 Peter 1:10–12)

- How does this help us in our approach to the Bible?
- What does it tell us about the way in which the Old Testament looks ahead to Jesus' death and resurrection?
- Where has God the Father raised Jesus to?
- How do the crowd respond to Peter's sermon?
- What response does Peter call for?
- What does he say God will give to those who respond?

Jesus: the life changer

ENDNOTES

1. Jesus read from Isaiah 61:1–2.
2. Luke 1:19–20, New Living Translation.
3. See Isaiah 40:3.
4. See Matthew 3:7.
5. This was the Holy Spirit, who had taken the form of a dove—see Matthew 3:16.
6. Matthew 3:17.
7. Joel 2:24.
8. Amos 9:13.
9. 'Solitary place' in Mark 6:32 literally means a wilderness place.
10. See Mark 6:34.
11. Malachi 3:2.
12. Mark 14: 6.
13. Matthew 16:23, New Living Translation.
14. See Mark 3:1–6.
15. See John 1:29.
16. John 14:6.
17. John 20:25, New Living Translation.
18. John 20:27.
19. 1 Corinthians 15:6.
20. Acts 2:25–27

About Day One:

Day One's threefold commitment:
- To be faithful to the Bible, God's inerrant, infallible Word;
- To be relevant to our modern generation;
- To be excellent in our publication standards.

I continue to be thankful for the publications of Day One. They are biblical; they have sound theology; and they are relevant to the issues at hand. The material is condensed and manageable while, at the same time, being complete—a challenging balance to find. We are happy in our ministry to make use of these excellent publications.
    JOHN MACARTHUR, PASTOR-TEACHER, GRACE COMMUNITY CHURCH, CALIFORNIA

It is a great encouragement to see Day One making such excellent progress. Their publications are always biblical, accessible and attractively produced, with no compromise on quality. Long may their progress continue and increase!
    JOHN BLANCHARD, AUTHOR, EVANGELIST AND APOLOGIST

Visit our web site for more information and to request a free catalogue of our books.
www.dayone.co.uk

U.S. web site:
www.dayonebookstore.com